The New Chalet School

The Chalet School series by Elinor M. Brent-Dyer

Elinor M. Brent-Dyer

The New
Chalet School

ARMADA

The New Chalet School
was first published by W & R Chambers Ltd,
London and Edinburgh.
First published in this revised Armada edition in 1975

Armada is an imprint of the Children's Division,
part of the Collins Publishing Group,
8 Grafton Street, London W1X 3LA

Printed and bound in Great Britain by
William Collins Sons & Co. Ltd, Glasgow

Contents

*Dedicated to Lucy Violet Moore of India
with love from Elinor*

CHAPTER 1

The Staff Meeting

"Hello, everyone! Had good holidays?"

"Splendid, thank you. And you?"

"Rather! My family greeted me with open arms, and I was *quite* the pet of the house. Pity it lasts such a short while!" And Miss Edwards, youngest member of the Chalet School staff, sank into her chair at the far end of the big staff table, and beamed round on everyone. "Why this solemn conclave?" she continued. "Is anything wrong?"

Miss Wilson, science and geography mistress, shook her head. "No; at least not as far as I am aware. But I came up only this morning, and haven't had much chance to discuss anything with anyone yet."

"Well, we shall all know soon," said her great chum, Miss Stewart, who, as she was wont to say plaintively, spent her life trying to drive some history home to the brains of the Chalet School girls. "Here comes Hilda at last! Come in, my child. What an age you have been!"

The door had opened to admit the Senior mistress, Miss Annersley. She closed it behind her, and came quietly to take her seat at the head of the table. The mistresses sitting round it looked at her, and then glanced at each other. Something *was* clearly wrong – and badly wrong, too. Miss Annersley's pleasant, clean-cut face wore a look they had rarely seen there. This meeting had been convened for more serious purposes than the usual staff arrangements at the beginning of term.

"What's wrong, Hilda?" asked Miss Wilson, voicing the question they all were longing to ask.

"I have two or three important things to tell you," said Miss Annersley slowly. "As you've all guessed that we've had trouble of one sort and another, I needn't bother to break the news gently."

"Oh, please don't keep us in suspense!" exclaimed Miss Stewart. "What is it?"

"I don't intend to." Miss Annersley nodded as she spoke. "I know better. First of all, Mademoiselle Lepâttre isn't returning."

There was a sudden silence. Then Miss Wilson spoke. "Not returning! Why not? I thought she was making such good progress. Surely nothing has gone wrong since we broke up?"

Miss Annersley nodded again. "I'll tell you what I know – it isn't much more than the bare facts – and then you'll all be satisfied on that score. Mademoiselle has made no progress this past week or two. She has, indeed, gone back. You know how ill she was the term before last. We – I feared then that we should lose her. However, she began to pull round, and everything seemed hopeful. Even after what the doctors said, I hoped she would be able to come back in time, even though it must be a long time. Now they say that she must give up all hopes of working again. It's no use glossing over facts. She may live for years – but it will be as an invalid."

Again that stunned silence. The staff at the Chalet School was a very united one, and they all loved their Head, Mademoiselle Lepâttre. A dangerous operation in November of the previous year had taught them just how dear she was to them. For some days the doctors had refused to say which way her illness would turn, and when, at length, she had seemed to set her feet firmly on the road of life again, her colleagues had all rejoiced fervently. They had known that her progress must be slow, so they had been quite content with it. Dr James Russell, husband of her partner in the school, and head of the great sanatorium on the Sonnalpe above the Tiernsee where the Chalet School is situated, had assured them that, humanly speaking, it should be only a question of time before their Head was with them again. Now, something had gone wrong.

Having given them time to recover from the blow, Miss Annersley went on. "Ten days ago, I was cabled for to come at once. Luckily, I was in Rome, and was able to fly to Innsbruck, so I wasn't long on the way. When I got to the Sonnalpe, I found that two days after the school broke up Mademoiselle had had a return of pain and sickness. They got her over that, but it came again, worse than before. When she was better the doctors had a consultation, and they now say that the mischief is more extensive than they had thought. If she could stand it, they would operate again, and a second operation would certainly put everything right. But her heart is too weak. All they can do is to mitigate the trouble as far as possible with injections and other treatment. This will prolong her life, probably for years; but they cannot cure her. And she must always, as I said, be regarded as an invalid."

"But – can *nothing* be done?" broke in Miss Wilson.

"No more than they are doing," replied Miss Annersley. "Oh, Nell! Don't you think they'd have done *any*thing if it had been any use? They have had men from Vienna and Bonn, as well as Sir James Talbot from London, and a

9

very clever surgeon from New York who is staying here for a holiday. They all agree that if they dared operate, the trouble could be set right. But – she would never live through a second operation."

Miss Stewart took up the tale. "Does this mean, then, that she'll go home to Paris? Or will she stay up at the sanatorium? Oh, Hilda! Whichever way it is, it's awful!"

Again there was a silence. Then Mademoiselle Lachenais, the modern languages mistress, spoke. "But, Hilda, what will Mademoiselle do? We all know here that she has nothing but what she earns. And then, she has helped her cousins, the Lecoutiers."

"We needn't trouble about that," said Miss Annersley. "The Russells will see that she does not want. And as for the Lecoutiers, Simone will, in two years' time, have finished her course at the Sorbonne, and come here to teach. Renée's education is secured here, of course; and when she is sixteen, she is to go to the Paris Conservatoire for training. Her music is very good. And then Mrs Russell suggests that Monsieur and Madame Lecoutier should take one of those large chalets they are building on the Sonnalpe and let rooms to visitors. They would be near Mademoiselle – and Simone, when she returns. And there is much need for *pensions* up there, as you know."

"That's like Madame," said Miss Edwards thoughtfully. "Yes; that would certainly seem to solve all difficulties so far as Mademoiselle and the Lecoutiers are concerned— "

"But not for us," finished Miss Norman, Head of the Junior school at the Chalet. "Hilda, what on *earth* are we going to do for a Head?"

"Madame and Mademoiselle have offered me the post," said Miss Annersley shyly. "I said I would accept if you all agreed."

10

A chorus arose at this. "*Agreed*" – "Mais pourquoi pas?" – "Oh, talk sense, Hilda! D'you expect us to go on strike?" – "Good for Madame and Mademoiselle!"

Miss Annersley turned red with embarrassment. "I wish I could think so. I'll do my best, and saints can't do more; but I'm not Madame, *nor* Mademoiselle. I'm glad to know you'll all back me up; I'll need it, I can assure you!"

"Oh, rubbish!" said Miss Wilson breezily. "You've run the school this last term and a half, and nothing has happened. Indeed, for us, we've been remarkably tranquil. Why on earth shouldn't things go just as well if you are *actual* instead of *acting* Head? You know we'll back you up to the last ditch."

Pretty Miss Stewart put in her oar. "And it isn't as if you had to begin with a perfectly fresh staff. I grant you *that* might take some doing. But we've all worked together for ages now, and we've never had any real trouble among us."

"No-o," said Miss Annersley doubtfully.

"Ma chère, what then is wrong?" Mademoiselle Lachenais added her quota. "Is it the girls you fear? I think you need not. They are all fond of you, and will do their best for you."

"Oh, be quiet, all of you!" broke in Miss Annersley, exasperated at these well-meant efforts to give her confidence. "You don't understand! You haven't heard all the news yet!"

"*More* news? Good Heavens! Let's have it and be done with it, then!" ejaculated Miss Wilson, while the rest of the staff eyed their new head with interest.

"Did any of you hear anything about Miss Browne last term?" asked Miss Annersley.

"Miss Browne? Miss Browne of Scholastika's, you mean?" asked Miss Wilson. "Not a thing – except that some of the girls were leaving at Easter, and she had none so far to take their places. I expect that's all right, though. There have been several new people up there, so Joey told me when she wrote last week." She nodded towards the window through which they could see the great mountain on the upper slopes of which lay the green shelf where stood the great sanatorium of which Dr Russell – Dr Jem, to the school – was head.

The faces of the staff changed. The Sonnalpe was a big item in the lives of the Chalet School and its friendly rival, St Scholastika's. Many of the girls in the two schools had relations "up there", as they always called it, and it was one reason why both had flourished.

Seven years ago the Chalet School had been started by Madge Bettany – now Mrs Russell – with only eight pupils. During the years, it had grown till it numbered some hundred and sixty girls, and not only paid for itself, but provided a steady if small income for its two partners. Naturally, such a school cost much to keep going and up to date. St Scholastika's was originally an English school, brought to the Tiernsee by its Head, Miss Browne, as an experiment three years before. The experiment had been successful, for while the Chalet School accepted girls of all nationalities and creeds, St Scholastika's was Protestant and took only British children.

The two schools had begun with a decided antipathy, but that was a thing of the past, and now they were firm friends, sharing many of their out-of-school interests, and joining in friendly rivalry over games. The two staffs were as friendly as the pupils, and, indeed, had regarded the feud at the beginning with amused consternation.

Mercifully, that had all come to an end. Now they waited with deep interest to hear what Miss Annersley could possibly have to say about Miss Browne and St Scholastika's.

"Do you mean to say," she began, "that you never heard about that lawsuit business of hers?"

Miss Wilson nodded. "Of course we did! At least, Con and I did, anyhow. We had to listen to the sad tale of 'my great-uncle and his bitter quarrel with my poor grandfather' the whole of one weary afternoon about two years ago – remember, Con?"

Miss Stewart nodded. "I remember. I was nearly asleep before it was ended, and Nell would keep on pinching me *sub rosa*. My arm was black and blue over that affair."

A laugh ran round the staff at this piteous tale. Then they grew grave again as Miss Annersley rapped on the table.

"Order, please! It's getting late, and I want to finish."

"Carry on! We'll be good!" Miss Wilson laughed.

"Well," said Miss Annersley, "the lawsuit has been decided in favour of Miss Browne's branch of the family. There is only herself left, so she comes in for what remains. I believe that originally there was a huge fortune; but you know what lawsuits mean. Still, she will have something like fifteen hundred a year when everything is settled up. She wants to give up her school, therefore, and go back to England."

"I don't blame her – at her age," said Miss Nalder, the physical training mistress, decidedly. "She must be verging on the sixties if she's not already there."

Miss Annersley nodded. "And then she's never taken to our winters. Altogether, this money will be a godsend to her. But you can't just drop a school like a hot potato, so

13

she's offered it to Madame and Mademoiselle – I believe at a mere nothing – and they have accepted her offer."

The staff sat in stunned silence on hearing this news. Characteristically, Miss Wilson was the first to recover.

"They have accepted? Then that means – "

"It means, in the first place, that we are enlarged this term by over forty girls," said Miss Annersley.

"Good gracious! How on earth are we to manage?"

"Well, naturally, we need a much larger staff. Equally naturally, the old St Scholastika's staff have been asked to join us. Miss Leslie left us last term, so we should have had to get a new maths mistress, anyhow. Madame and Mademoiselle knew about all this last half term, and they asked Miss Soames if she would carry on here. Then Miss Anderson is coming for English. I can't go on giving my usual lessons when I have all the organization on my shoulders, as you may imagine – Jeanne," she smiled at Mademoiselle Lachenais, "Mademoiselle Berné will help with the modern languages and Latin – unless you like to do as Madame suggests, and give up all the French classes and keep the Latin in your own hands."

Mademoiselle Lachenais laughed. "I cannot decide such a question at once, Hilda chérie. I must think it over. But I am glad Julie Berné is coming here. I like her, and I think she will be a very pleasant colleague."

Miss Annersley nodded and then turned to Miss Norman. "Ivy, we have asked Miss Phipps to join the Junior staff. You will have ten new babies from St Scholastika's, and you have a fairly big number as it is. You know her quite well, don't you?"

Miss Norman chuckled. "My dear, we've supported each other through one of the worst crossings from St

Malo that I ever remember. I'm glad to have May Phipps. She's a dear!"

"Then," continued Miss Annersley, "we really have needed another resident piano mistress, so Miss Elliott will solve that trouble nicely. And finally, another matron now becomes a necessity, and Miss Rider will fill that place – Matey," she turned to Matron Lloyd, head of that side at the school, and beloved and feared by girls and mistresses alike – "I know you and Gertrude Rider are chums, so I hope you are pleased."

"An excellent choice," said Matey calmly. "She's a woman of sense and won't try to ride roughshod over everything that doesn't suit her tastes exactly."

There came another burst of laughter at this, for the year before the school had been inflicted with a matron who had been the reverse of this, and it would be hard to say whether staff or pupils most rejoiced when she took her departure.

"Yes; all this sounds very nice," said Miss Wilson when order was restored. "But you have forgotten one very important thing, Hilda."

"What's that?" asked Miss Annersley quickly.

"Why, where in the world are we to put all these people?"

"I say!" exclaimed Miss Edwards. "That's going to be rather a problem, isn't it? We're overcrowded as it is."

"We are," agreed Miss Wilson. "Of course, I can take about twenty more at St Clare's if we use those two unused dormitories. And there are three bedrooms for staff. But more than that I couldn't get in with a shoehorn! So now what?"

"Well, we must manage as best we can for this term,"

15

said Miss Annersley. "But by next term we hope to have a new house. The men started to dig the foundations last week, and it ought to be ready by the end of September. And that reminds me; it has been decided when it is finished to make changes in organization all round."

"What on earth d'you mean?" demanded Miss Stewart, sitting up at this. "I hope you aren't going to take us three away from St Clare's – that *would* be a blow!"

"You needn't worry about that," returned the new Head. "You three will remain there, of course. But it has been decided that, next year, instead of having the various stages separate they are to be mixed. There will be Seniors, Middles and Juniors in each House for the future."

"Oh!" exclaimed Miss Norman. "How simply awful!"

"Why? You will have prefects among your girls, naturally. And the House prefects will be given as much responsibility as the school prefects. I don't think you need worry, Ivy. I know you had a bad experience last year; but that was exceptional. And, in any case, Miss Phipps and Dorothy here will be with you. With four prefects and three staff the girls certainly can't go very far wrong."

"Some of those Middles could go wrong if they had the whole hierarchy of angels on guard," murmured Miss Norman sceptically.

"Don't be so flippant, my child," said Miss Wilson calmly. "And if you feel as bad as that about it, why not see Madame and ask to be removed from the position of house mistress?"

Ivy Norman shook her head. "And admit that I'm incapable – for that's what it would amount to! Oh, no thank you, my dear! No; I must stick it, and hope for the best – that's all."

"And where will the rest of the staff go?" inquired Mademoiselle Lachenais.

"You know that chalet a hundred yards south of us? Well, it has been bought, and the land between it and our grounds, and it is to be a staff hostel, where all of the staff we can't fit in at school will live. Mademoiselle Berné will be there, and Miss Elliott, Miss Carey, and Fraülein Felsen. And then we have engaged a Miss Greene for Junior English, as you'll have enough to do with the babies, Ivy, and she will live there. Frau Mieders is giving up her flat in Innsbruck and coming, too, and she will be head of the hostel. And as Madame thinks we ought to honour an English saint, it is to be dedicated to St Hild" ("Who's she?" murmured Miss Edwards), "and the new House will have to be St Scholastika's."

"Is that all?" asked Miss Wilson.

"Isn't it enough?"

"Not quite," said Miss Nalder suddenly. "When are the new staff arriving? You haven't told us *that* yet."

"They will be here tomorrow, and we shall have our ordinary staff meeting tomorrow at twenty o'clock. That will give us all the weekend to settle down and get accustomed to each other. The girls will be here on Tuesday as arranged before."

"I wonder what they will think of it all?" murmured Miss Stewart, as the Head arose to indicate that the meeting was at an end. "Nell, wouldn't you like to be a fly on the wall in some of their homes just to hear what's being said?"

"Not in the least," said Miss Wilson serenely. "And if that's all the comment you can make, I think you'd better come with me to the lab and apply such brains as you have to helping me make out a stock list. – You *did* say all stock lists had to be in by Frühstück tomorrow, Hilda, didn't you?"

"Yes; Miss Denny is going in to Innsbruck and will call here about ten for them. So have them ready. And, while I think of it, do try to write distinctly, Nell! You know what a bother we had last term about your supplies."

Miss Wilson grimaced at her, but acknowledged that her writing might easily be more legible, as she followed her new Head out of the room.

"Better come to us for lessons in script," called Miss Norman after her. "I'd *love* to teach you something, Nell!"

"I dare say! I'll come to you for script if you'll come to me for chemistry," was the answer that floated up the stairs to them. "Is it a bargain?"

But Miss Wilson did not even wait for an answer. She knew that Miss Norman hated science in any shape or form, and, with a jolly laugh, she caught Miss Stewart's hand and raced her through the corridors to the laboratories, which lay at the far end of the school.

CHAPTER 2

The New Plans

The girls of St Scholastika's were nearing their destination and the new term. This was nothing fresh, of course. What *was* fresh – to many of them, at least – was the fact that they were coming to the Tiernsee to join a new school. It is true that they and the other school were already friends, but, though they were friends, they had had no thought of amalgamation, and to some of them the new arrangement had been a decided shock.

"Whatever put it into the Fawn's head to retire?" demanded Hilary Burn, a tall, pretty girl of sixteen-and-a-half, as she sat in the railway compartment with her great chums Ida Reaveley and Nancy Wilmot. "I thought she had no existence apart from St Scholastika's."

"I suppose it's that money business," said Ida thoughtfully.

"Well, I'm still gasping about it," rejoined Hilary. "Mother told me about a week ago, and I've felt as though I were under a cold shower ever since – when I've thought of it, that is."

Nancy laughed lazily. "What? All the time? How chilly you must feel! I got a shock myself, but I've recovered now. I'm rather interested in what's going to happen next. I've always liked all I knew of the Chalet School, and I think, so long as the Fawn has given up, it'll be jolly good fun joining them."

"It will probably mean a good many changes – for us," said Ida. "Have you ever thought, Hilary, that you would have been our Head Girl next year if St Scholastika's had carried on? It's not likely you'll be asked to fill that position at the Chalet School."

"Thank Heaven, too!" said Hilary fervently. "I was dreading it. I'm one of the youngest of our crowd, remember. Only your cousin is younger, Nance. I know you'd all have been decent and backed me up, but the younger ones mightn't have seen it in the same light. I've no desire to have to deal with criminals like Betty Wynne-Davies and Elizabeth Arnett by myself, thank you!"

19

"We'd soon have sat on them if they'd tried to play you up," said Nancy.

"I'm sure you would! But I'm not so sure that it would have been the right way to go to work. Some of those kids simply turn obstinate when you sit on them. Gypsy tried it last year, and you know what happened then."

They assented. The said Gypsy had had a hard time with certain members of the Third and Fourth Forms who had organized a little clique of their own with very definite ideas, and two capable leaders in the said Betty Wynne-Davies and Elizabeth Arnett.

"Gyp was a dear, but she wasn't too tactful," said Ida.

"Tactful? She doesn't know the meaning of the word! But those kids gave her an awful time of it. She never dared to ease up for a moment. Now I should hate that. I like to take life easily – as easily as one can when one's Sixth Form, with all the work and responsibilities and so on of these days."

"I wonder if any of us will be prefects?" mused Nancy. "We may not – we really are new girls, you know, though it isn't what's usually meant by 'new'."

"Oh, I expect some of us will be called on to take duty," yawned Ida.

"Oh course we shall," declared Hilary vigorously. "I'm certain they won't make me Head Girl; but I'm equally certain they'll appoint some of us as prees. For one thing, the school is sizes larger than it was last term. They'll need more prefects. And they'll think we'll know how to handle our own people best."

"I hadn't thought of that," acknowledged Nancy. "Oh, dear me! I was looking forward to a nice lazy term, with no responsibilities at all."

"Lazy object!" said Ida scathingly. "No wonder you're so fat!"

Nancy chuckled with exasperating good humour. She was not sensitive about her bulk, and always pointed to her elder sister, who in her teens had been as fat as she herself was at present, and was now possessed of a slim elegance delightful to behold.

"I wonder if Mademoiselle Lepâttre will be back?" said Hilary, changing the subject quickly. There were times when Nancy irritated Ida to the verge of rage, and the youngest of the trio had no mind that they should enter their new school with a squabble.

At her words, the young faces grew grave for a moment. They had all known Mademoiselle Lepâttre, and all liked her. When the news of her illness had reached them during the previous Christmas term, they had been very sorry, and very anxious to hear the daily bulletins which were phoned to them at their own request.

"I doubt it," said Ida at length. "The last I heard, she wasn't expected to return till September at soonest. She was awfully bad at Christmas, you know."

"Who told you?" asked Nancy.

"Elsie Carr. I travelled home with her and her father. Mr Carr had to go to England unexpectedly on business, and he took Elsie with him for company. Don't you remember I was stuck at school three days after the rest of you left with that stupid throat? Mr Carr heard of it, and offered to escort me to Dover, where Dad would meet me. Elsie told me then that Mademoiselle was not expected back till September."

"Then that would mean Miss Annersley as Head. I like her," said Nancy definitely.

"Oh, so do I. If you come to that, I like all their

staff that I've met."

"Haven't they lost that jolly maths mistress of theirs?" asked Hilary.

"Yes; she left to be married," replied Nancy.

"Perhaps they'll take on Soamesy for maths then," suggested Ida.

Hilary made a face. "What a horrid suggestion! Oh, Soamesy's all right out of school hours; but in them she's a ghastly nuisance. I wish maths had never been invented!"

"Hear! Hear!" said Nancy. "In my humble opinion all maths people are the extreme edge!"

A girl went down the corridor just then, pausing to flash a smile at them through the window, and Hilary, seated by the door, pushed it back and summoned her imperiously.

"Anne Seymour! Don't go galloping off like that! Come in here and cheer us up – do! We're feeling awfully blue at the thought of being new girls all over again at our age."

Anne, a slender, pretty girl of seventeen, looked at them and laughed. "You look it! Wait a minute, and I'll come back. I've got to go and count the Middles just to be sure that none of them was left behind at Innsbruck. I won't be a second, and then I'll come and try to brighten your moments."

She nodded gaily to them, and then ran down the corridor, to return five minutes later and occupy the vacant corner in their compartment.

"Now then," she said, when she was comfortable; "what do you want to know?"

"Well, first of all, why are we ostracized by all your crowd in this way? Two or three of them peeped in here, and then passed on. I can understand Middles; but why can't Seniors join up with us? Don't you like the idea of our coming in with you as a school?" Hilary looked anxiously at her as she spoke.

Anne laughed. "You goose! Of course we like it! The school will be all that much larger, for one thing. But we decided that you'd probably like to be together to discuss this – this strange event in all its entirety before we barged in on you. Therefore, we left you to it. And now you accuse us of ostracizing you! So are one's good intentions misunderstood!"

They all laughed. Then Hilary said, "I see. But we've had oceans of time for private discussion, and now we want some encouragement. Tell us all about you."

"Tell you all about us? Why, you know us quite well!"

"Only as outsiders. Now we are to be insiders, and we'd like to know a little more."

"Well, what *sort* of things do you want to know? Are we nice? Though I say it as shouldn't, we're quite nice when you get to know us."

"How modest! No; that isn't the sort of thing. Give us some idea of what's expected of us in the way of work and behaviour," said Ida. "What are the most important rules?"

"Let's hope they're not too strict, or some of our little crowd will be in for a peach of a time," said Hilary. "Certain of our Juniors are the limit for behaviour. I'm warning you in good time so that you'll know what to expect," she added kindly.

"They couldn't be worse than some of ours," declared Anne. "We've one or two bright stars among the Middles that would make most folks' hair rise. Alixe von Elsen and Mary Shaw, for instance."

23

"You haven't met Betty Wynne-Davies and Elizabeth Arnett yet," said Hilary darkly.

"Which are they?" asked Anne with interest.

"Elizabeth's a kid with red hair and a pale face – looks too good to be true but is a perfect little fiend on occasion. I'm surprised at *any* school taking her. I'm sure she put years on to the Fawn's life! And Betty Wynne-Davies is worse. She's a regular gypsy of a kid – black eyes, black curly hair, and a brown skin. She *does* the bad things; Elizabeth *thinks* of them."

"Not that Betty needs any encouragement in that line," added Ida. "That kid was born to be hanged!"

"Or murdered!" Nancy supplemented the remark. "You'll soon know all about them, Anne. Look out for a pair of innocent-looking darlings with the colouring Hilary describes. And remember that the more innocent they look, the worse you may be sure they've been."

"*Another* of those!" groaned Anne. "As if Alixe von Elsen wasn't more than enough for any school!"

"What? Have you one like that, too? Oh, help! What a flowery time we seem to have before us!"

Anne glanced quickly at Ida, the last speaker. "I say, Ida, there is one way in which you'll have to reform yourself, my child, and that is language. I may as well warn you now."

"Oh, my aunt! What do you mean? Have we to talk German or French all the time?"

"Oh, no; we have a day for each language – we're trilingual, you know. But what I meant was that we're not allowed to use slang – or not much, anyhow."

"I remember now," said Hilary. "When we were getting ready for that sale of work we had last year, your Miss Annersley overheard some of us talking, and she

24

said, 'Not so much slang here, please. We don't want our Juniors to pick it up.' I wasn't saying anything so very awful, either – nothing like what I *could* do once I got going!" She smiled impishly at them. "What happens if you use too much? Let's hear the worst."

"Fines," said Anne succinctly. "It soon runs away with your pocket money, and being penniless isn't a situation that appeals to *me*."

"It certainly doesn't to me! I say! What a rosy prospect lies before us!"

"You're not very comforting, Anne, my child," said Ida in dismay. "What are the other rules?"

"Oh, just the usual things about not talking on the stairs or in the corridors. And then we have to remember what day it is – "

"*What?*"

"I mean if it's English, or French, or German. I told you we had a day for each. Then we begin all over again. On Sundays, we all talk our own language, though."

"What a simply awful outlook! I look like being dumb except for Sundays!"

"Oh, it's not so bad as it sounds. When you hear a language being spoken all round you, and nothing *but* that language, you soon pick it up," said Anne consolingly.

"Not this child! I've been here three years now, and I don't speak German a great deal better than I did when I first came – blankly ignorant of a word."

"Ida Reaveley! Aren't you ashamed to confess it?" demanded Hilary. "I'm no great shakes, of course, but I can get about if I must."

Ida laughed. "You have to have a gift for that sort of thing, my child, and I haven't got it."

"I've heard other people say the same thing," said Anne. "When you have had a few of Bill's patent remarks you'll soon find you can get on if necessary – and it *is* necessary at the Chalet."

"I wish I could think so! My people *would* rejoice! But I'm afraid the heavens will drop before that happens. Hello! Is this Spärtz we're coming to? Where has the time gone?"

"Where time usually goes, I suppose. I must fly. I'm responsible for seeing that six little darlings get safely out of the train with all their belongings. If I'm not there, they'll probably leave half of everything behind, and we shall keep the train waiting past schedule time, and then they won't love us! So long, you three! See you later!" And Anne left them to go and perform her duty.

The three others gathered together their possessions, and when the long Innsbruck-Kufstein train drew up beside the station, they were able to jump out quickly, pile their luggage on the hand truck awaiting it, and then go to the help of the Juniors.

Four mistresses were in charge of them, having come to Innsbruck on escort duty, and two more were waiting on the Spärtz platform. But in spite of this, it took them a good ten minutes to get every girl and her belongings out of the train and safely herded across the platform to where the little mountain railway went up to the Tierntal from the Inn valley. However, it was done at last, and Miss Wilson and Miss Stewart watched the girls climb up into the little open carriages, while their colleagues, who were in already, saw to it that all were properly bestowed.

"Isn't it early this year?" said a voice behind the "new" girls.

"It's only running today because of us," replied another

voice, strongly tinged with an American accent. "Guess they'll shut down for another fortnight once the last of us is safely landed."

"How do you know that, Evvy?"

"I saw Madame when I was up at the Sonnalpe last week, and she told me they'd arranged this because there's oodles of us this term, walking would be a puzzle. So they're running *two* trains – one now, and another about eighteen o'clock for the late girls."

"What an honour!" laughed the first speaker.

Hilary, standing behind Ida and Nancy, glanced in the direction from which it came, and uttered an exclamation, "Gillian Linton! I thought you'd be up at the Sonnalpe! What are you doing here? Is Joyce with you?"

The girl she addressed, a slender, very pretty person, with long black plaits, eyes of pansy-blue, and the pink-and-white colouring of a fairy-tale princess, gave an exclamation and joined them.

"Hilary! What fun to see you! What did you think of the news?"

"Never more flummoxed in my life. Seems imposs that we're going to go up to the Tiernsee and not see the Fawn. What about you?"

"Oh, I've had a week or two to get accustomed to it," laughed Gillian. "Madame told us almost as soon as it was definitely arranged. She came to tell Mummy – you know how we all try to give her every scrap of fresh news there is to cheer her up."

"How is she?" questioned Hilary anxiously. "I do hope she's better."

Gillian nodded. "Oh, much better! But the weather has been bad, and it is so depressing when you see nothing but white clouds or streaming rain, day after day.

27

Madame understands, and she knew that such an event as the Chalet School and St Scholastika's amalgamating would keep her interested for days. Joyce and I were there when they were discussing it, so we heard it. We've talked about it from every single point of view, I should think – Yes, Miss Wilson; we're coming." For Miss Wilson was beckoning them impatiently to the train.

They climbed in and took their seats, and Gillian went on: "I was simply thrilled, and Joyce is wild with excitement. And Mummy was so interested that she quite forgot the weather. It's been better yesterday and today, and she's been out in her chair, so it's all right."

"But if you were at the Sonnalpe, how is it you've joined us now?" queried Nancy.

"I've been spending the weekend with the Mensches. You remember Frieda Mensch, don't you? She asked me to spend a few days with them, and I had to go to see Herr von Francius – a stopping came loose – so I took the opportunity and went."

"Will Joey be there to welcome us?" asked Anne as the little train puffed importantly on its way, and began to move across the narrow space that lay between the station and the mountain slope.

Gillian shook her head and looked mysterious. "She *might* be – I can't say for certain. But I quite expect to see her – if she and Madame haven't been too much taken up with their new summer home."

"New summer home? Gillian Linton, what do you mean?" demanded Anne.

"Yes; explain yourself, my child," commanded Ida. "What new stunt is this?"

"Oh, just the very latest," said Gillian airily. "I only heard it myself from Jo on the phone to Frieda."

"Gillian, if you don't hurry up and explain, I'll shake you!" vowed Anne.

"Don't do that – Bill might see and tick you off," advised Gillian. "Oh, all right! I'll tell you. I can see you'll all burst before we get up if I don't!"

"Well?" asked half a dozen voices impatiently as she paused.

"Why, Dr Jem has bought St Scholastika's, and they are going to use it as a summer home. Joey will be down by the lake practically the whole of this term. How's that for news?"

"Topnotch!" It was American Evvy who spoke first. "I always knew Dr Jem was bully, and I guess this is the best yet."

"When will they be down?" asked Anne.

"As soon as possible. Joey and Madame were coming down today to see it, and to take measurements for carpets and curtains and so on. Joey said that, if they weren't too busy, they'd probably stroll round to Seespitz to meet our train, at any rate."

"Gee! Some news that!" And Evvy (otherwise Evadne Lannis) bounced in her seat with satisfaction.

"Don't bounce like that, Evvy!" protested Anne. "It's enough to send the train over the edge."

Evadne chuckled and subsided, and for the rest of the slow journey up the mountainside the girls discussed this fresh piece of news with a vigour and enthusiasm which showed their feelings towards Madame and Joey. Finally, the little engine uttered a defiant hoot, surmounted the last of the slope, and sped valiantly across the valley to Seespitz, the Tierntal terminus.

The girls who knew were keeping an eager lookout, and at sight of two figures standing by the little shed that serves as a station, they raised a cheer. Not even the mistresses could have kept them from springing out of the carriages and racing across to where a slender, graceful woman with a delicate, elusive beauty of her own stood by the side of a tall, black-eyed girl, whose thick black hair was wound in coils over her ears, with a broad fringe cut straight across her brows, shadowing a delicately cut, mobile face, full of interest for anyone who was skilled in character reading.

"Joey!" Gillian was there first, though most of the rest were not far behind. "This is simply topping! And you, too, Madame! How lovely to see you both again!"

"And how gorgeous of you to meet us!" added Anne.

Mrs Russell laughed. "Oh, you'll be seeing lots of us this term. I expect, seeing you've Gillian with you, you've heard the news. We shall all be coming round, and expect you to come to us, as well."

"You bet we will!" cried Evadne. "Oh, blow! There's Bill calling! We must go, but gee, I'll tell the world this is going to be one grand term!"

And with this final speech, cramful of forbidden slang, she tore off in answer to Miss Wilson's frantic whistling. The rest followed, and the pair who had come to welcome them were left alone.

Joey turned to her sister and raised her eyebrows. "I wonder?" she said. "What do you say, Madge? Think it'll be all jam, as Evvy so confidently prophesies?"

Madge Russell laughed. "Oh, not quite so wonderful, perhaps. People will have to shake down and get used to each other. There's all the new staff to fit in. And then they'll probably learn some time that Mademoiselle will return to school no more." Her face saddened. "They won't like that, Joey."

30

"No; but *will* they be told this term? I thought no one would say anything."

"They aren't stupid. Some of them will guess. And Gillian *knows*. I am convinced of that. Well, it's no good talking, Jo. We must get back to St Scholastika's and join Jem and the Robin. I expect he's waiting for us, and rapidly losing his patience over us. Come along!"

"Jem never did have much patience," declared his young sister-in-law as she followed her sister. "I wonder what he'll say when he hears *our* latest? He'll probably go off the deep end when he hears what's been done to you. Sisters-in-law don't matter so much. But wives— "

"Wait to tell him till we get home," advised her sister. "And don't waste time chattering, Jo. We ought to have been ready for him twenty minutes ago."

"Only we couldn't miss the girls," supplemented Jo cheerfully. "All right. But I do wonder what he will say!"

CHAPTER 3

The Children at the Hotel

In order to link up this story, it is necessary to go back a few hours. Dr Russell had motored his wife, her sister, and his little ward Robin Humphries, down to the lakeside shortly after breakfast, or Frühstück, as they were accustomed to calling it. The three girls wanted to go over the new summer home and take measurements for curtains and rugs, and see how they would settle the rooms. He left them, promising to come back for them about fifteen o'clock, and bidding them be sure to have a good meal at one of the many hotels which have grown up round the lake in the past fifty years.

"Don't you worry about that. We'll see to it all right," Jo assured him as he got into his car again.

"And don't let Rob get overtired," he added to his previous remarks.

"As if we should! You run away and get on with your own jobs, and leave us to ours!" retorted his sister-in-law vigorously.

He laughed and drove off, leaving them to enter the big chalet and make a survey of it. Then, leaving the Robin upstairs, dancing in and out of the rooms, and trying to decide which she would prefer for her own, the sisters descended to what had once been a form room, and Madge Russell flopped down on a broad window seat while Joey took the centre of the floor, hands in her blazer pockets.

"Well?" Madge looked up questioningly at Jo. "What about it?"

Jo glanced round the big room. "Not too bad. We'd better make this the salon – I wish it had French windows, though. We shall miss them after Die Rosen."

"It's only for a few weeks, and if I know anything of the family, we shall be out of doors most of the time – unless we get very wet weather. It's in quite good order. If we have the walls colour-washed cream – I couldn't have my salon that awful shade of green— "

"Equally, you couldn't have a form room cream," retorted Jo with a grin. "You're right about changing it, of course. It's a most bilious hue. We'll make it cream as you suggest, and have curtains, etc., of some of that vivid floral cretonne we saw in Herr Hamel's window last week. That will make it bright enough. Then the old Speisesaal will do for us – also with a few renovations. The Fawn seems to have gone in exclusively for that *useful* verdant shade, doesn't she? Then what used to be the girls' common room can be the day nursery, and if you'll take my advice you'll leave it as it is."

"I've had a brilliant idea," announced Madge, getting up and going to the door. "We'll get some of those sheets of nursery-tale figures, and cut out the pictures and paste them up."

"Then I hope you'll put them well out of the babies' reach," said Jo. "Otherwise, they won't last long."

Madge laughed. "Come along and let's look at the room."

The sisters strolled down the wide hall, arm-in-arm, and stopped in the doorway of a large, sunny room, colour-washed in what Joey had called "that *useful* verdant shade". It had two large windows of the casement type, and a big, covered-in stove, so was safe enough for little people. Two huge cupboards with glassed-in upper doors and wooden lower ones filled up opposite corners. The floor was of parquet, easily kept clean, and broad, low window seats ran along beneath the windows.

"Those will be useful," said Jo, waving her hand towards the cupboards. "The babies can keep their toys in the bottom parts, and the nursery crockery and Rosa's sewing materials can be kept in the upper ones."

Madge nodded. "That's what I thought. And what used to be the prefects' room will do for a sitting room for you and the Robin. You must talk it over with her, and see what you would like done with it. It will give her something fresh to think about."

Joey assented soberly. They were all anxious to keep the Robin's mind filled with pleasant thoughts. Motherless since she was six, she had lost her father, Captain Humphries, the secretary to the Sonnalpe, early that January. He had taken a mountaineering holiday, in company with Dr di Bersetti, one of the Sonnalpe doctors, and the pair had had an accident, with a rope breaking, and precipitating both down the rock face of the mountain they were climbing. The young doctor had been killed immediately, and Captain Humphries so gravely injured that it was plain he could not live.

Dr and Mrs Russell had flown to him from Innsbruck, and had been in time to hear his last wishes. He had forbidden them to bring the Robin, saying that he wanted her to remember him as she had known him in life. He left her to the Russells, knowing well that they would guard her as well as he could have done. The few possessions he had were in the doctor's care, and he would be her guardian till she was twenty-five.

With tears in her eyes, Madge Russell had promised him to give his little daughter all the loving mothering she gave to her own small pair and her brother's children, also left in her charge, since Dick Bettany was in the Forestry in India, and the climate was not suitable for white children. He gave her hand a quick clasp, as he was then beyond speaking, and turning a little, slipped away to the country where the wife he had adored was waiting for him.

The Robin was a frail little mortal, and there were always fears lest she should have inherited the cruel "white man's plague" which had carried off her mother. But, fortunately for her, she had been trained to obedience, and had never been permitted to fret. She mourned for her

34

father, but she knew that he was happy with her mother now, so, with her usual sweet submission, she tried to be her own sunny little self; and as the Russells were very good to her, her health had not suffered as much as they had feared. But they were all thankful for anything that would help to take her thoughts off her loss. Mercifully, Dr di Bersetti had left a young wife behind him, and Bette, an Old Girl of the Chalet School, had faced up to her loneliness with such courage that even the Robin, baby as she was, had been impressed with it. Besides, Bette had a little son; and in the April, a tiny sister had come to join him. The young widow had not only given her baby the Robin's real name – Cecilia Marya – but she had also called on the little girl for much help.

So, although there were times when the child sobbed out her longing for her father, they were becoming rarer. This idea of decorating the nursery themselves would give her plenty to think about, and plenty to do, and Joey agreed cordially that it was an excellent idea.

"And the little common room for you and Rob, as I said. We must alter that, too. What do you say to a sunshiny yellow?"

"Good scheme! Which room will you have for the night nursery?"

"The big dormitory above this, I thought. The room next door will do for me and Jem, and there's a tiny one opening out of it that will serve him for a dressing room. Then the little dormitory for you and Robin, and the Matron's room for Mamzelle Rosa will sleep in the night nursery as usual, of course. I can curtain it off."

"What about furniture?"

"Jem suggests getting wickerwork as far as possible.

We'll paint and varnish the floors, and get some cheap, pretty rugs for them. After all, we want it for a summer home only. Muslin curtains at the windows, a few pictures, and heaps of flowers will make it pretty."

"And a few books to give it a lived-in appearance," supplemented Jo the bookworm.

"André can make a couple of sets of shelves, and we'll have a selection of our favourites down here."

A clatter of feet on the uncarpeted stairs put a stop to the sisterly duet as the Robin came rushing in to ask excitedly which was to be *her* room?

"You and I share the little dormitory," said Joey, smoothing back the thick black curls from the lovely little face. "I say, Madge, what about Rosalie? Will she be here, or will she stay up at the Sonnalpe?"

"Oh, here, of course. Jem will be down as much as he can manage, and he couldn't have his secretary up in the mountains while he was down in the valley. She can have one of the little bedrooms at the far end of the corridor, and what used to be the stockroom for an office. I'm arranging the other big form room as Jem's study, and she ought to be near him. In her free time, she'll share your sitting room. The rest can be guest rooms. We're certain to have shoals of visitors once we settle down. Now, Jo, help me measure the windows for curtains. We'll do what we can till half past twelve, and go to the new hotel for Mittagessen. After that, we'll finish measurements, and then stroll along and meet the girls. By that time, Jem ought to be back, and we mustn't keep him waiting. Rob, you get that notebook from my bag and write down what I tell you, pet."

The next hour was a busy one as they measured all the upstairs windows for curtains, and paced the rooms to get some idea of the number and size of rugs they would need. They were so busy that it was quite a surprise when Jo, happening to glance at her watch, announced that it was half past twelve already, and as they had to tidy themselves before they could go to any hotel, they had better get on with it at once. Tape measures were put away, and the three hastily attended to their toilettes. Then, all very spick and span, they came out of the chalet, locked the doors behind them, and sauntered along to the new hotel, which had been built only that summer.

A burst of music greeted them as they entered, and Jo made a face. "Jazz band!" she murmured to her sister with disgust.

Madge shook her head. "Not likely up here. Radio, I expect. You'll have to put up with it, Joey. Come along! Here's the Speisesaal."

In the Speisesaal, or dining room, the proprietor appeared to welcome them. He knew her, of course. Most people in that district knew the gentle, lovely wife of the brilliant young doctor who was head of the sanatorium at the Sonnalpe. The Tyrolean bustled forward, ushering them through the long, sunny room to a dais where there were three tables plainly set apart for anyone of special importance. One was vacant, and the man drew out the chairs with many bows.

Smothering her dismay at this very public welcome, Madge took her seat, and Joey and the Robin followed suit. The menu was brought, and they chose their dishes.

"I feel painfully conspicuous up here," observed Joey as she unfolded her napkin. She gazed round the room. "I say! They seem to have got going pretty rapidly. Quite a number of the tables are filled."

Madge nodded. "Mainly family parties, I see. Look

37

at those children over there – twins, obviously."

Jo glanced across the room at the dark-eyed children who were regarding them with deepest interest. "Italians, from the look of them," she said, lowering her voice carefully. "I wonder who the lady is with them – not their mother, I'm certain. She looks years too old."

"There are some more over there, Joey," said the Robin, nodding her head in the direction of two pretty children of ten or eleven, who were sitting on either side of a young clergyman. A pretty woman, obviously mother of the three, faced them, and the whole party looked very happy.

"What throngs of children they seem to have here!" said Joey, looking round. "There's a small boy over there; and another boy and a girl at that table in the far corner. You may make friends of some of them, Robin, when we come down. You'll not have Amy, or Laurenz, or Daisy, except for occasional weekends, you know."

"They're only visitors. Probably they won't be staying any length of time," said her sister warningly.

"You never can tell. They may be here with people at the sanatorium. Didn't Jack Maynard say last night that seven new cases had come? Perhaps these are some of their belongings. Der Goldene Apfel is full up at present, and there isn't a room to spare at any of the private places. The sooner the Lecoutiers get here and open, the better, I should say! They'll be full up in no time."

"It will be so nice for Renée to have her father and mother here," said the Robin wistfully. "But it will be triste for Simone, all alone in Paris, n'est-ce pas?"

"Simone will have too much to do to think about it, and she's coming out for the vacations," said Madge. "You may be right, Jo. However, we should be settled here in about ten days' time, and we shall soon know. Jem wants us two to go to Innsbruck tomorrow to get what we need in the way of furnishings. We'll get bare necessities to begin with, I think. The luxuries can come later."

"All right," agreed Jo. "Well, if those children are here for some time, Rob will soon get to know them, and then she won't feel lonely. I want to get on with *The Rose Patrol in the Alps*, and there ought to be a chance here. The school can't visit us without permission, and we won't get people dropping in at any hour of the day, for we haven't many acquaintances hereabouts – not till June, anyhow."

"Good idea," said Madge. "Here's our soup at last! I'm famished, and we still have a good deal to do before we go back. By the way, Jo, remind me to ring up Tante Gretchen when we get back. They will give us Mittagessen tomorrow, I know."

"*And* Kaffee and Kuchen," supplemented Jo, savouring her soup with the air of a connoisseur. "I say; this soup isn't bad, is it?"

"It is *good*," said the Robin, with one of the turns of speech that reminded them that she was half-Polish, and French her mother tongue. "Tante Guito, may not I come, too?"

Madge looked at her thoughtfully. "Yes; if you will go straight to Tante Gretchen's and wait there. Shopping would be too tiring for you, my pet."

"And you can keep Tante company, for I'm going to ask Frieda to come with us," said Jo.

"That's a good idea, Jo. I'm afraid Frieda sometimes feels – Good gracious! What *is* the matter with you?" For Joey had suddenly emitted a suppressed squawk, and was pressing a hand to her cheek.

"Something hit me on the face," Jo looked bewildered. "It stung horribly. I believe I'm bruising. See!" And she removed her hand, and presented her cheek for her sister's inspection.

Madge looked anxiously. Sure enough, there was a discoloration coming up on it. Under her tan, Jo had a white skin which bruised easily, and the blow had evidently been a sharp one.

"Here! Rub some butter on it!" Madge passed the dish. "It's a nasty place. What can have done it, I wonder?"

While Joey rubbed butter on the place, her sister looked up at the ceiling, for she could think of nothing but falling plaster to account for the blow. But the ceiling looked perfectly smooth and sound. And meanwhile Joey, with well-greased cheek, was looking for a napkin to wipe her buttery fingers. Herr Schmidt was hurrying up with one, and offers of a lotion for the cheek, which Jo politely refused.

"It is all right, mein Herr. The butter will prevent discoloration," she said in her fluent German.

"But I cannot understand," mourned Herr Schmidt. "What can have caused it? It is not plaster from the ceiling, gnädiges Fräulein, for that was well done, and is of the best plaster."

" 'It was the *best* butter,' " murmured Jo to Robin, who promptly giggled. Then she turned to the distracted hotel proprietor. "Perhaps something has loosened just a little, mein Herr. No, indeed, there is no need for lotion. See; is it not fading already?"

Herr Schmidt examined her cheek almost tearfully. What a terrible thing to have happened to the sister of the ever-to-be-reverenced wife of the great Herr Doktor who was such a power at the Sonnalpe! He had put all his

40

money into this venture, and hoped to do well; but if such things occurred to the Herr Doktor's relatives, would he not warn the friends and relations of his patients against the Seehaus?

It was ten minutes before Madge and Joey between them managed to calm down the little Austrian. They succeeded at last, and he departed to warn his waiters to see that the gnädigen Damen at the table on the dais should have no cause for complaint.

The three settled down to enjoy their delicious lake trout, and discuss furnishings, the Robin putting in her small oar at intervals. The fish was followed by a delectable entrée. Then came the sweet, a trifle made of boiled chestnuts beaten with sugar, whipped cream, and crescents of crystallized tangerines gleaming goldenly against the ivory hillocks of the cream.

"How gorgeous!" said Jo greedily, as she tasted. "I could make a meal of this!"

Then she dropped her fork, for Madge had uttered a cry, and was pressing her hand to one temple.

"Tante Guito, what is it?" demanded the Robin, jumping up. "Oh, Joey! Tante Guito bleeds!" And she went white.

Sure enough, there was a tiny cut on the temple, from which a thread of blood was trickling. Mercifully, Herr Schmidt was out of the room at the moment. Otherwise, as Jo said when they were discussing it later on, he would have succumbed to a fit.

"Hush! Say nothing!" said Madge quickly, as she wiped away the blood with her handkerchief. "Go back to your seat, Rob; I'm not killed. Jo, what *is* the matter?" For Joey had uttered a triumphant sound, and suddenly dived at her sister's lap to pick up something.

"There you are, my dear!" Jo held it out. "*That's* what hit you! And I suppose mine was the same. Some little beast has been catapulting us!"

Madge glanced at the tiny pellet of lead on the palm of her hand. She was angry now. "I don't mind an accident. But this sort of thing is beyond a joke. Have you any idea who it could be? If I knew, I would certainly let Herr Schmidt know. This sort of thing won't bring him visitors, you know."

Joey allowed her gaze to move round the room. Most people had not seen the second incident, and were going on with their meal. But at the table below them, well to the right, the little boy she had guessed to be Italian was sitting looking at them, and it seemed to her that there was a wicked triumph in his glance, though he looked away the instant he caught her eye. His sister was not so quick, and she blushed and giggled. Their father – he was plainly that – was reading, and took no notice of them, and the elderly lady was absorbed in her sweet.

"I can't say for certain, Madge," said Joe, "but I wouldn't mind betting that it was that imp of a boy down there. His sister knew all about it, for she went beetroot and giggled when I caught her eye. But you can't say anything, of course. Giggles and beetroot blushes aren't evidence. All the same, I propose to keep an eye on the pair of them." And she did so, greatly to the discomfiture of the pair, who wriggled at intervals for the rest of the meal.

Jo noted that they were pretty children with their dark, liquid eyes, black curls, clear olive skins, and small, well-cut features. Both had the same determined chin, and both were clad in white woollen sweaters and white shorts.

"Twins for a ducat!" she said to Madge and the Robin when the party finally moved away from the table. "Also imps. That young man deserves a jolly good spanking – and his sister, too."

"Well, there's one thing certain," said Madge, as she gathered up her bag and gloves. "We won't come here again in a hurry if we're to be exposed to that sort of thing. There are limits!"

She settled the bill, and then the three went back to St Scholastika's and worked hard till near the time when they knew the first mountain train was due.

"We'd better make ourselves tidy," said Madge, pushing back her ruffled hair from her face. "I feel a mess, and Jo's no better. Jo, I hope you've got a comb with you? Your hair is *awful*!"

Jo sighed as she unpinned the thick coils of plaits over her ears. "Hair is a nuisance. If you have it short, half of your allowance goes in getting it cut. If it's long, it never looks fit to be seen. I wish I could wear a wig! It would save me an awful lot of trouble!"

Madge laughed unfeelingly as she took down her own black curls, and shook them free. "Rubbish, Jo! If you'd only learn to put in your hairpins properly, you'd have no trouble. *I* never have any worry."

"Your hair is down to your waist, and curly into the bargain," Jo pointed out. "Mine's straight as a barge pole, and not much past my shoulders, even yet. Why on earth I couldn't have had curls, too, passes my comprehension."

"Give me your comb and I'll do it for you," commanded her sister.

Jo handed over the comb, and Madge proceeded to manipulate the refractory locks, pinning the numerous short plaits – Jo's hair was exceedingly thick – round and round, till they lay in two great flat shells over her ears. Then she combed out the Robin's riot of curls, and finally attended to her own.

"Three crows' heads," said Jo as she took back her comb. "We must look as if we'd all used the same tar barrel."

Madge laughed. "Rob's hair has reddish lights in it; and mine isn't as black as all that. Yours is the only really *black* one among them. Oh, listen! There goes the engine whistle! We must hurry, or they'll arrive before we do."

"The train's far enough away," said Jo, hastening her steps nevertheless. "It won't be up for some minutes yet."

"Still, we don't want – *Oh!*" Madge stopped short with the exclamation. A pellet had flown past her face, almost grazing her nose.

"This is beyond a joke!" exclaimed Jo, making a dive into the thick brush that clothed the land up to a tiny alp which was kept for hay.

There was a rustling, and faint cries. But Jo was long of leg and sure of grip. Three minutes later she reappeared, hauling along a small boy. He turned his head as they reached the path, and Madge saw that the captive was the small boy that had been in the Speisesaal at the Seehaus. In one hand was a catapult; the other was engaged in pommelling Jo, who easily defended herself and dragged him up to her sister.

"Here he is!" she cried. Then, with a sharp shake, "Now then, you little wretch, just beg pardon at once!"

The boy stood obstinately silent, though his fine eyes were glowing with rage. Thoroughly roused, Jo gave him another shake, with no more effect than before. On the instant, there was a crashing through the bushes, and his sister appeared, long curls flying, face white, eyes flashing. She flung herself on Jo with clenched fists, and had not Madge kept her wits about her, the trio might have gone over into the lake, for the path was narrow here, and Jo was taken by surprise. As it was, Mrs Russell just managed to prevent the catastrophe by dint of grabbing the young lady round the waist and hauling her to one side by main force.

"You silly baby!" she said scornfully. "Do you want to drown the three of you?"

"I don't care – she has no right to shake Mario – let me go – let me go till I kill her!" gasped the child in Italian.

"Stand still," said Madge sternly. "Do you hear me?"

She spoke the same tongue, and either the shock of hearing her own language, or else force of personality took effect. The child ceased wriggling and stood sullenly still.

Seeing his sister's attitude, the boy, too, stopped struggling, and Jo and Madge and the Robin stood round the pair.

"Why did you shoot at us at Mittagessen?" demanded Jo the ready.

No answer; though she had spoken in Italian.

"Why did you?" she repeated.

Still no answer.

Then she acted. Letting go of the boy's shoulder, she snatched the catapult from him, and snapped off the prongs. At sight of his toy's destruction, a cry broke from him.

"You've broken my catapult! How dare you? How dare you? My papa will send for the gendarmerie, and you will go to prison!"

"Don't talk nonsense!" said Jo contemptuously, as she flung the fragments into the lake. "And another time, do try to behave like a gentleman if you can!"

The effect of her last remark on both children was startling. Spitting out her words, the girl snarled, "How dare you! How dare you speak to us like that – us – di Balbinis! Our father is a prince— "

"Nonsense!" said Jo flatly. "I suppose you mean your father's a member of one of the princely families of which Italy seems to produce such dozens. But that doesn't make you *royal*! Talk of dukes being four a penny! I should consider such specimens as you cheap at a soldo a gross!"

The boy flung round on his sister. "You hear, Maria! She insults us!"

"She shall pay for it – they both shall!" retorted Maria through clenched teeth.

"Children!" said Madge. "That is not the way for you to talk. As for who you are, we don't know. We can judge only by your behaviour, and that is scarcely the behaviour of royalty. Now run away and be thankful that we do not complain to your father. If such a thing ever occurs again, I warn you, I shall do it. Run along now."

She released Maria as she spoke, and the child sprang out of reach. "We hate you, and we will pay you both out – both of you!" she shouted at the top of her high, clear voice. Then she caught her brother's hand. "Come, Mario!"

Still holding hands, the pair raced off down the path, only pausing when they were well out of reach, to turn and make a sign that roused Jo to yearnings for a cane and the right to use it.

46

"The little brutes made the horns at us!" she cried. "And then they talk of 'insults'! Witchcraft, indeed! I only wish I *were* a witch! I'd soon teach that promising pair a lesson!"

"Hush, Joey," said Madge gravely. "If they are wrong, so were you in saying what you did about dukes and princes. It was both cheap and childish, and I'm surprised at you."

"Well, they made me wild," apologized Jo. She knew her sister was right.

"And so you lowered your dignity because of what a pair of poor, silly babies said and did? I thought you were grown-up now."

This was scathing; but Jo passed it over for the moment. "Madge! What do you mean? You sound as if you knew them."

"So I do. They are the children of Prince and Princess Balbini. Two days ago their mother was brought to the sanatorium in very bad shape. Their father adores her, and thinks only of her. The children have been left to the care of his elder sister who, is, so I hear, a gentle creature, as well fitted to deal with a cageful of lions as with those two. They have been allowed to run wild, and, I suppose, think they can do what they like. They don't know about their mother's condition, for their father thinks them too young to be told. Jem told me so."

"All very well," said Jo, as she turned and accompanied the other two across the water meadows. "But if all the children at the new hotel are like those two demons, I think it will be just as well if Rob tries to content herself with us. – Hello! There's the train! Come on!" And she broke into a run as she saw the train, whistling deliriously, come hurrying across the little plain to the Seespitz station.

CHAPTER 4

"Who Did That?"

When Mrs Russell and Jo had vanished, the girls formed into long files, and were marched along the western shore of the blue Tiernsee. A broad path ran round the lake here, with water at one side and the mountain wall at the other. In one place the mountain retreated, and here stood a large chalet, where a tethered goat was feeding in the small garden. As the school marched past, he lifted his head and emitted a contemptuous bleat at which the girls laughed.

"Heinrich doesn't seem any more friendly with us than he ever was," said Anne cheerfully to Hilary, with whom she was paired. "He's a most scornful creature."

"He looks a bit vicious," said Hilary, casting back a glance at Heinrich, who was eyeing them malevolently.

"I shouldn't like to say he isn't: Luckily, he's never free, so there's not much danger. I've heard that goats can be really nasty."

Hilary laughed, then she glanced across the lake to where stood the big chalet which had housed their former school. "How nice of the Russells to take St Scholastika's for their summer home! I've had three happy years there, and I'd hate to see it standing empty and forlorn."

48

"You know we're to have another house built, don't you?" asked Gillian, who was behind them with Ida. "That was another piece of news Madame gave us."

"Oh good! But what are we to do this term?" asked Anne.

"Squeeze in, I suppose. I've heard nothing about that."

"Oh, well, I expect we shall hear all about it at Assembly," said Anne comfortably. "Has Lulu come yet, d'you know, Gill?"

"I don't know. She was up at the Sonnalpe when I went down to Innsbruck yesterday. Her brother has been ill again. He's getting better now, though."

"Poor Lulu! What a time they've had with Leonard!" said Anne, with a sympathetic thought for the Chalet School Head Girl, who was her own great chum. "Oh, look! They've taken in that little chalet – Felsenheim, isn't it? The wattles go right round. Why's that, Gill?"

"It's to be a staff house, I believe," said Gillian. "I can't tell you more, though. Wait till Assembly, and then you'll know."

By this time the path had opened into a wide, tri-angular valley which ran back from the shores of the lake to the mountains. Dotted about were sundry chalets and big hotels, for the Tiernsee has become a tour-ist centre. A high, wattled fence with a broad, deep ditch running round it shut off the various houses from view – and also helped to keep inattentive people from wasting time. A wide plank bridge crossed the ditch to the gate, with handrails at either side, and a big PRIVATE fastened at one side. The gate stood open, showing glimpses of a hedge of climbing roses trained on five-foot trellises. Trellis arches crossed it at inter-vals, also rose-covered, though at present the vines bore only young spring foliage. The girls passed up the path under the arches, and entered by the big, wide-open door.

Hilary found herself in a cool, shady hall which she knew very slightly, since, on her previous visits to the school, she had used the side door common to the girls. But on the first and last days of term everyone came in by the front door which was usually sacred to staff, prefects, and visitors.

A tall, pleasant-faced woman – Miss Annersley – came swiftly along the hall to meet them. "Welcome, every-one," she said. "Have you had good journeys? – Anne, Louise is at St Clare's, longing to see you – Evadne, I believe you've begun to grow! What a relief! Cornelia is upstairs in Green where you and she are this term, together with Suzanne Mercier and Polly Heriot – Where are Hilary Burn and Nancy Wilmot?"

"We're here, Miss Annersley," said Hilary, coming forward.

"Ah! Such a crowd of you makes it difficult to see you all at once," smiled Miss Annersley. "I'm very glad to welcome you to the Chalet School, and I hope you'll be happy with us. You two are in the Green dormitory, too. Evadne can take you up there now, so that you may settle in at once. Now," she went on, as Evadne departed, towing Hilary and Nancy after her, "I'm going to read out the names of the girls who are to be at St Clare's. Anne, you might take them with you, and hand them over to Miss Wilson."

"Yes, Miss Annersley," said Anne.

Miss Annersley read out the names of twenty-seven girls, and then nodded to Anne who, with a brief, "Come along, everyone!" led the way round a turn in the hall that took them to the long corridor which linked up St Clare's with the main building.

"The Juniors are all at St Agnes', of course." went on the Head, referring again to her list. "Is Arda van der Windt there?"

"Here, Miss Annersley," and Arda, a very pretty Dutch girl of seventeen, with long black curls and black-lashed grey eyes, came to the front.

"Arda, I want you to take the little ones to Miss Norman who will see to them. One moment, dear! What is the last news of your father?"

"Much better. The doctors think that in another six months he will be completely cured. It was only a threatening, you know."

"I'm so glad, dear. Now I'll read out the names, and you might take them to their own house. Gillian will go with you, as there are rather a number of them." Then Miss Annersley read out the names of the twenty-three small people, who meekly lined up beside the two big girls and followed them from the hall.

Only a group of four girls was left now – Ida Reaveley, Ernestine Emery, a pretty fourteen-year-old, with coppery-red hair, eyes like sapphires, and rose-petal skin, Dorothy Hatcherd, mousy-brown of locks and sallow of colouring, with clever, grey-green eyes behind enormous spectacles, and Viola Emery, a younger sister of Ernestine's, and very like her. There were also, near a window, four of the old Chalet School girls – Gianetta di Patelli, Giovanna and Anita Rincini from Innsbruck, and Jeanne le Cadoulec, a Breton girl. These four formed a little coterie of their own, having come up through the school side by side almost since its inception. Miss Annersley beckoned them to her, and they came at once.

They hoped to hear that they would be together, and not have to share with anyone. However, they were doomed to disappointment.

"You eight will share the Yellow dormitory, with Ida, who is a prefect, as Head," said Miss Annersley. "Joyce Linton will have the ninth cubicle, but she will not be down till eighteen o'clock. Anita, lead the way, dear. Your names are pinned to the curtains of your cubicles so you can make no mistake."

"Ja, mein Fräulein," said Anita, speaking in her own tongue.

Miss Annersley laughed. "Forgotten all your English during the holidays, Anita?" she teased. "Let's hope it comes back before tomorrow."

"I beg your pardon," said Anita, flushing. "I forgot for a moment."

"Oh, run along, all of you! Anita, can't you learn to know when people are teasing?"

Anita looked dubious, but Miss Annersley waved them off, and so she turned, with Gianetta at her side, and led the way upstairs to the big, airy dormitory, where Ida found herself in a pretty cubicle, hung with primrose-coloured curtains, and with primrose-covered duvet on the bed. The rugs were yellow to match, and the big window had yellow curtains.

"How awfully pretty!" she exclaimed. "And what a lovely view of the lake!"

"It is always the prefect's cubicle," explained Anita pleasantly. "I have the other window, so I suppose I must be second-in-command."

"What does that mean?" asked Ida, as she took off her hat and coat and hung them away in the big cupboard at one end of the room which Anita pointed out to her.

"Only that when you are late at prefects' meetings I must be in charge. Shall I show you the bathroom? You will want to wash your hands."

"I should think so! A complete bath would be more the size of it. I do wish they wouldn't use that awful soft coal on the engines!" said Ida as she followed her guide.

Anita laughed. "But they always do. Yes; I know it is dirty. But you do not look bad, Ida. Will you come back to the dormy when you have washed? I must go and hang my hat and coat in the cupboard."

She vanished, and after a good wash which made her feel fresher, Ida returned, to find them all ready to go downstairs, and pleasantly anxious to show her the way.

Hilary and Nancy joined her as soon as she entered the common room, and while Anita and her chums slipped into their own special corner, the St Scholastika girls formed a little threesome beside one of the windows and sat discussing the situation.

"We unpack after tea," said Hilary, when second cups of coffee were being filled. "Then we do as we like till Assembly, which comes at seven. After Assembly, we have supper – no; what do they call it here? Some weird German name, I know. It means supper, anyhow. After that, all over fourteen can dance till nine – or twenty-one as they say. Then bed – and I shan't be sorry to get there. What a treat it will be to sleep in a decent bed again after two nights in the train!"

"The journey's the only real snag about coming to school out here," agreed lazy Nancy. "I tried to get the pater to let me fly, but he wasn't having any. I must say, considering he's so mad keen on it himself, he might have been more open to persuasion. If he can go up and do all sorts of mad stunts, and try to thrash around in what-d'ye-call-it? – the – the – "

"The stratosphere, I suppose you mean," interrupted Hilary. "Perhaps that's just why he won't let you."

"Why on earth he should want to sit on his che-ild's aspirations towards flight, I can't think!" grumbled Nancy. "I'm dying to go up, and I've never even had a joy ride."

"He probably thinks there isn't a plane built that would stand your weight," teased Ida, with a glance at Nancy's buxom figure.

"Insult added to injury!" yawned Nancy. "Oh well, I *should* worry! Fat runs in the mater's family, and I'm like them. I can't help it."

Meanwhile, in another corner of the room, the Head Girl, Anne Seymour, Paula von Rothenfels, and Arda van der Windt were all gathered together, discussing Mademoiselle Lepâttre very seriously.

"But what is the *real* news of her?" asked Arda. "*When* does she return? Lulu, you spent your holidays up there, while I was in Haarlem. Do you know what they say?"

Louise Redfield, a handsome, dark-eyed girl from New Orleans, shook her head. "Very little indeed. I know she hasn't been so well lately, but Dr Jem told us there would be ups and downs. It's practically over, though, and maybe she'll have fewer as time goes on. I'm sure I hope so. Don't you fret, honey – Mademoiselle – Ow! Atishoo! *Atishoo!* ATISHOO!"

She concluded her speech with a series of violent sneezes which made her quite incoherent. But in the disturbance that arose no one had time to notice. All of them were sneezing, and as they groped for their pocket handkerchiefs, their eyes streamed, and they choked and gasped. No one noticed that the little oriel window at one end of the room, which had been darkened momentarily, was now clear again. No one saw two small figures slide down the great chestnut which grew just outside, and go streaking across the garden and out at the side entrance. No one heard one of the pair remark to the other as they finally pulled up, breathless, by the white wooden fence that marked the beginning of Briesau, "There! That will give them something to think about! It is *their* school – Herr Schmidt said so! The sister of a schoolteacher to dare to shake you, Mario! We will make things so horrible, that all the girls will want to leave, and then they will have no school left. Wasn't I clever to think of the snuff?"

To which the other person replied with a chuckle. "I hope it will take lots and lots of things like that to make them go away. It was fun to hear them all sneezing!"

No one at the school was thinking of anything at the moment except that they were all afflicted by some fearful epidemic of sneezing. However, they gradually recovered, and when Miss Annersley, Miss Wilson, and Miss Stewart all came to inquire what on earth was the meaning of the pandemonium, they obtained an answer. It came from Evadne Lannis' friend, Cornelia Flower, another American, famed for her enormous blue eyes, her bright hair, her square chin, her habit of getting into scrapes, and her outrageous language when she was roused – as at present.

Spluttering between sneezes and fury, Corney, as everyone called her, burst out, "Some mean, rubber-necked hind-footed *glumph* has gone and chucked oodles of pepper or snuff or something all over! I guess I'd just like to know who it is! I'd darn well show them!"

"Cornelia!" Miss Annersley's voice was very quiet, but it brought the orator to a stop, and she turned a rich purple and began to stammer apologies, while her friends stuffed their handkerchiefs into their mouths in their endeavours not to explode in the mistresses' faces. Corney had certainly outdone herself this time.

Meanwhile, Anne and Louise, searching for the cause of all the fuss, had reached the oriel which stood wide open, and something attracted Louise's quick eyes. She pulled a chair along, and climbed up, holding her handkerchief over her nose and mouth. Evidences of a raid were plain to be seen. Snuff lay along the windowsill in little heaps, as if it had been accidentally split. What was more, someone had found a burst paper bag on the floor, and a darkish patch on the whitewash of the ceiling helped them to construct the crime. Some agile criminal had climbed the chestnut – they found signs of that, too, when they went round to examine it – and, leaning in at the window, had flung a crammed bag of snuff up against the ceiling, bursting it, and causing the terrible sneezing attack which had incapacitated everyone for a minute or two.

Just *how* the girls had never noticed what was going on, it was impossible to say. Miss Annersley thought they must have been too much absorbed in all their chatter to heed the darkening of the oriel. As to who had had the daring to think out and execute such a plan, that was a problem that was not likely to be solved in a hurry.

But this did not prevent the entire school from going about for the next few days as one animated question mark after the sentence, "Who did that?"

CHAPTER 5

A Fresh Mystery

The origin of the snuff remained a mystery. Miss Annersley made a few pointed remarks about the silliness of practical jokes of the kind in her speech at Assembly, which took place an hour or two later; but she left it there. This was the first day of term, and there was always a little licence permitted on the first day.

But when she had finished with the episode and passed on to tell the girls that Mademoiselle Lepâttre would not come down to the school for months to come, there were groans. Mademoiselle was plain, not too chic, a stern disciplinarian on occasion, but the girls loved her dearly, and even the girls at St Scholastika's had liked her enough to join in the outcry. Had they known the full truth – that her teaching days were over – there might have been more than groans. But those in authority had decided that the girls should not know everything yet. Let them get accustomed to knowing that Mademoiselle was at the Sonnalpe and in bad health. The news that she would never again be their Head would not come as such a shock in a few months' time. This was what had been decided, and Miss Annersley said as little as she could.

She explained that present arrangements in the school would next term be altered, and instead of being divided into Senior, Middle, and Junior houses as at present, so many of each division would be drafted off into the four houses they hoped to have.

"We don't want the Juniors to feel cut off from you elder girls; nor do we wish the elder girls to feel they have no responsibility for the little ones," she said. "We will finish the year as we are, but after that things will be different."

"Glad I shan't be here then," whispered Anne to Louise. "I've always loved our present arrangement. I don't know that I should be so very keen on having all ages mixed up."

Louise nodded, and then turned to listen again, for Miss Annersley, having paused, was continuing.

"I have a piece of news that will please you, I think. Dr Jem has taken St Scholastika's, and is to use it as a summer home. He, Madame, Joey, the Robin, and all the babies are coming to it as soon as possible. Some of you elder girls will remember Rosalie Dene, who was one of our girls for a short time. She is now at the Sonnalpe as the doctor's private secretary, and will come with them. Madame told me that she hopes you will all go and visit them. As for Jo, I gather we may expect to see plenty of her. I am sure she won't be able to stay away when it means only a short row or a pleasant walk to reach us."

A cheer broke out at this. The girls were fond of Joey Bettany, who had been Head Girl of the Chalet School for four terms, and had taught a good part of the succeeding term, while the various episodes of her earlier schooldays were already passing into legend. Joey, as Miss Wilson could have told you, had not been a peaceful person to have in a school!

The Head waited for the cheers to subside, and then turned to Miss Wilson, now first mistress in the school, since Miss Anderson, who was to be senior English mistress, had come there only that term. "And now, Miss Wilson, will you please read out the form lists, as you have them?"

Miss Wilson rose at once. She was a very tall, athletic-looking woman, with a clean-cut face, dark brown hair which rippled over her head in silky waves and was fastened in a great knot at the nape of her neck, keen grey eyes, and a chin which rivalled that of Cornelia Flower. She was a great favourite with her pupils, despite her reputation for sarcasm, which made evildoers dread falling into her hands. Without being pretty, she was good to look at – fresh, and crisp, and very much "on the spot".

She began to read at once in a clear, rather deeply pitched voice, and the girls listened eagerly, for, with so many new girls, it was plain that there must be big readjustments of forms.

They were right. They had begun the year with two Sixths and two Fifths. Now there were to be two Fourths and two Thirds as well. The result was that certain little coteries in those forms found themselves broken up, and pulled long faces over it in private. Alixe von Elsen, for example, who could generally be relied on to keep things lively, found that she had been promoted to Five B, while Kitty Burnett and Emmie Linders, two cronies of hers, were still in Four A; Joyce Linton, another of their gang, had been moved up into Five A, so Alixe had not even the satisfaction of being with her.

Miss Annersley knew all about it, of course, and smiled to herself when she saw suddenly downcast faces. She knew that those crestfallen looks were not altogether because certain people were not promoted, and, though she said no more about it, she was still wondering if any of the girls knew anything about the snuff which had so mysteriously upset the Kaffee und Kuchen hour.

After form lists came prefect lists, and the girls found that, in addition to the former Chalet School prefects, Hilary Burn, Ida Reaveley, Irene Silksworth, and Nancy Wilmot were prefects. However, that had been expected, and roused little comment. Those of them who knew the four were quite pleased to welcome them among the grandees; and to the younger girls, prefects were prefects, and not unusually a horrible nuisance.

Miss Annersley said a few more words to remind them that though, for the first week, new girls would be excused if they spoke in their own tongues, yet after that they would all be expected to manage as well as they could in the language for the day. The Chalet School took girls of many nationalities, and it had been literally necessary for them to be trilingual, speaking English, French, and German with equal fluency. Miss Annersley warned the newcomers that they would be wise to do their best to keep the days with the others from the very first. Then she dismissed them, and at once a gong sounded, and while those in Ste Thérèse's, as the original house was called, marched off to the Speisesaal, the rest streamed away to the other two houses.

"Abendessen, thank goodness!" said Anne to Louise. "I'm so hungry I could eat an elephant!"

"I hope not!" laughed Louise. "There won't be much left for the rest of us if that's how you feel."

Hilary, left behind at Ste Thérèse's, turned to Gillian Linton, who was talking to her young sister, Joyce, a startlingly lovely girl of fifteen. She had just come down from the Sonnalpe, where their mother was living, since the doctors had all warned her that England meant death for her.

"You might show me the way," she said plaintively.

Gillian laughed. "Poor old new thing! All right, Joyce; I'll be over to St Clare's later on, and you can tell me the rest then. Anyhow, you ought to be there now. You'll get into trouble if you're much later."

"Not first night," said Joyce confidently. "All right; I'm going. See you later. Bye-bye, Hilary. Hope you'll like here." And she galloped off.

"I'm all frightened," observed Hilary as she and Gillian went to the Speisesaal. "However I'm going to manage to talk I can't think. My French isn't so bad – I might get along there. But my German is *awful*!"

"You'll soon pick it up," said Gillian soothingly. "I knew next to no German when we first came, but I can manage all right now. And if you get stuck, there's always someone to help you out. They aren't too strict the first term if they see you are really trying."

Hilary heaved a sigh like a groan. "I'll try all right. It's a nuisance not being able to do all your own shopping. They do understand English in the big shops; but in a little one, you're frequently done unless you can get hold of an interpreter."

"We'll help you out," promised Gillian. "Come and sit here, Hilary. Table lists haven't been made out yet, so we can sit where we like till tomorrow."

Hilary nodded after a glance round to see about Nancy. That placid young person was being looked after by Cyrilla Maurús, another Old Chalet Girl; and Ida was further down the same table with Cornelia and Evadne. She sat down in the chair beside Gillian, once grace was over, and they began the meal to the accompaniment of a perfect babel of chatter.

Naturally the talk turned first on Miss Annersley's speech, and then on the snuff business.

"Who did it I can't think," said Gillian, eating soup thoughtfully.

"It was a very dangerous thing to do," said Cyrilla severely. "It might have gone into our eyes, and that would have been very painful."

"It was quite bad enough when it went up our noses," declared a bright-faced girl of sixteen, whose bush of curly hair was for ever falling into her eyes. "I was weeping like a waterspout before I was through."

Evadne, overhearing, laughed. "Say! If ever I find out who the great slob is, you bet I'll make them sorry!" she said.

"Evvy! Your language!" cried Elsie Carr, a pretty, dark-haired girl sitting at the end of the table. "If Bill or Nanny heard you, you'd be fined, first night or no!"

"It takes real good American to express all we feel about it, I guess," said Evadne calmly.

After Abendessen, the girls danced until twenty-one, when a bell rang and they stopped instantly, and there was a hurried putting to rights of the room. The few girls who had still been unpacking came to join them and they formed into lines. Gillian pulled Hilary into place beside her, and then, at a word from Louise, the file marched out of the room and into another which Hilary recognized as one of the big form rooms.

"What's going to happen now?" she asked Gillian in a whisper.

"Prayers," replied Gillian.

"Don't we have them all together?"

"Of course not. We're Protestants; the rest are Catholics. We always divide for Prayers. The Abbess – Miss Annersley – takes us; and I suppose Bill or Charlie will take the Catholics. That's what happened last term, anyhow."

"I see. I hadn't thought of it before. Why do we come here, though?"

"Because there are always heaps more Catholics than Protestants, even now when you people have come. Before, we were a very small handful. Hush-sh-sh! Here's someone coming."

The door opened, and Miss Annersley came in. She was followed by all the former St Scholastika staff, with the exception of Miss Phipps, who had attended the St Agnes' prayers. One or two of the old Chalet School staff were there, too, but the majority, like the girls, were Catholics.

When Prayers were over, the mistresses left the room, and when the girls presently went upstairs, they found Miss Annersley standing at the foot to say good night to each girl individually.

"That's rather nice," decided Hilary as she undressed and brushed out her gleaming hair, which was at the uncomfortable stage of growing from a bob. "It makes you feel she takes a real, personal interest in you."

Then, for she was very tired after her long journey and all the excitement following, she slipped to her knees by the side of her bed and said her prayers, and tumbled into bed, asleep at once.

She was so tired that she slept straight on through the night. Indeed, she never stirred till the rising-bell sounded, and then she lay for a minute or two, looking at the white curtains sprinkled with sprays of green leaves, wondering where she was.

"Are you awake, Hilary?" asked Suzanne Mercier's voice, just as she had realized that she was at the Chalet School. "Please will you get up at once? You are one of the first on this morning's bath list."

Suzanne spoke in French, which was the official language for that day, but she spoke slowly and carefully, and, greatly to her surprise, Hilary found that she understood most of it. Later, she discovered that it was the rule always to speak so to new girls until they had mastered sufficient to follow with a fair amount of ease. Now, she jumped out of bed, and found fair-haired Evadne Lannis waiting for her, a gaudy orange spongebag swinging from one hand, and a huge bath towel slung round her neck.

"Dépêche-toi, Hilary!" said Evadne. "Il faut que nous nous dépêchons toujours le matin."

Hilary went with her to the bathroom at the head of the stairs, and when they were inside, found that it was divided into two neat little cubicles, each with its own bath, toilet basin, and hot pipes for towels. Evadne explained that she might have the water lukewarm if she chose, but not hot in the morning.

"I take it cold myself," she added, as she turned to the door, "but if you are not accustomed to it, it would be well to take the chill off. It's very cold at this time of the year, for the water comes from the lake, you see."

Hilary chuckled inwardly to hear the prim French, but declared that she preferred her morning bath cold. Evadne nodded, closed the door, and retired to the other cubicle, where Hilary heard her splashing at a great rate. Then she threw off her things, and plunged into the water, to emerge two minutes later glowing from its icy sting. A brisk towelling followed, and seven minutes after she had left the dormitory she was back, fresh, and wide awake, and as warm as toast. She hurried into her clothes, and when Suzanne came to fetch her, she was quite ready, bedclothes lying over the chair, bed shaken up, and only her cubicle curtains to toss over the seven-foot-high iron rail. That done, they went downstairs, where breakfast was the order of the day, although it was just seven o'clock.

"We always have Frühstück at once," explained Evadne. "Then there is a walk until a quarter to nine. After that, Prayers and lessons."

"Bedroom work is done before the walk," added Cornelia Flower, Evadne's compatriot and great chum. "If you take music, you must practise then, too. They started this plan last term after Cyrilla turned faint one morning because she had been working like a slave at her cello. Miss Annersley was frightened and sent for Dr Jem, and he said we had better have something to eat before we did any work. So now we have Frühstück as soon as we come down."

Frühstück was strange to Hilary. Miss Browne had kept up all English customs at St Scholastika's, but the Chalet School folk had followed the example of the country, and had rolls and bowls of milky coffee with a little fruit at the first meal. At eleven there was milk, or cocoa, and fancy bread twists. Mittagessen came at one – or thirteen, by continental time – and was followed by half an hour's rest on mattresses which were laid on the floors of the common rooms, when there was silence. After that, there were more lessons so long as the great heats of the summer did not come. Kaffee and Kuchen, the Tyrolean form of tea, took place at sixteen o'clock, followed by games until eighteen. Then they had preparation – an hour for the younger girls; two hours for the Seniors – and then Abendessen. After that, they were free to amuse themselves as they chose. Saturday was a whole holiday, except for the first hour, when they did mending, or wrote letters. Guide Meeting came at ten o'clock, and went on till noon. But after that, they were free again.

"Wonder what we'll do about Guides now?" mused Evadne during Frühstück. "We've two Companies already – we have to! There are fifty or more in each Company. And, of course, we have Rangers and Cadets as well. You Saints will probably keep yours, and that will give us three. What about Brownies, I wonder?"

"No idea," said Hilary. Then she broke off, for Miss Stewart, who had come over from St Clare's for breakfast, and was sitting at the staff table near by, was looking at her reproachfully.

"It strikes me I'll *have* to learn French and German, whether I like it or not," she thought, as she addressed herself to her roll. "I know we were supposed to have one French day a week at St Scholastika's; but I can't say it did me much good." Then she remembered that they had all with one accord fought shy of Mademoiselle's table, and had talked a curious polyglot which had passed for French. Evidently there would be no chance of that here!

After Frühstück they went upstairs to make their beds, and then they had to hurry down for the long walk which all must take except those girls who had to put in practice. Suzanne explained that they would stop work at eight-fifteen, and take a short walk. They took it in turns for this, so that no girl practised early in the morning every day.

With so many girls, they never went together, and

66

on this occasion, Hilary, who did not learn music, found herself with about twenty others walking briskly up the valley towards Lauterbach, the tiny hamlet at the head of the great Tiern Pass which runs through the mountains into Germany.

"This is new to us," she said to Paula von Rothenfels who had paired off with her. "The Fawn never brought us this way. We stuck to the lake, or else went down the mountains for our walks."

"Try to say it in French, Hilary," said Paula, who was a conscientious girl. "See, I will say him for you, and you shall repeat him after me. It is much easier if you try from the first." And she carefully turned Hilary's speech into French, and coaxed the English girl to repeat it after her.

Hilary shrugged, and laughed, but she was wise enough to know that what everyone told her was true, and that the more she tried now, the easier she would find it when the time came for slips to mean fines. Since she was a prefect, she was not liable for order marks as the rest were.

Behind her, she could hear Margia Stevens and Berta Hamel helping Nancy, who described herself as "the world's worst dud at languages"; and Gillian was doing the same thing for Ida.

Since many of them were prefects and all Seniors, they had no mistress with them; so when they elected to turn and come back by the lake – down the banks of the little stream which divides Briesau peninsula, and then past their own boathouse – there was no one to say them nay. Once they had reached the rails that shut off Briesau proper from the rest of the valley, they had to form ranks again, for rules were strict on this point. There were so many visitors to the Tierntal during the season

67

that the girls knew they must be on their best behaviour or they would bring discredit on the school.

"We shall just have time to look at the bathing shed and boathouse before we go in," said Louise, who, with Irene Silksworth as her partner, was leading them. "We mustn't be late the first day, or Miss Annersley *will* have something to say!"

They marched briskly along the bank of the brook which danced in headlong fashion down to the lake. Then they crossed the bridge, went past a small slated house which they knew as Wald Villa, the home of the large family whence the school and Die Rosen at the Sonnalpe drew most of their servants – Joey had once said, "there seems to be a never-ending stream of Pfeiffen girls coming along!" – and so down to the shores of the lake, just in advance of a long crocodile formed by the senior Middles, in charge of Miss Stewart and Miss Nalder, who were winding their way homewards after a delightful walk to what was known as the Dripping Rock.

The Seniors walked on sedately, turning aside when they came to the railed-off enclosure which held the two buildings. Louise, who had the key to the gate, unlocked it, and they streamed in, while she exclaimed, as she shut the gate on the last pair, "Oh, isn't it good to see them again!"

The Middles marched past, casting envious glances at their elders who were crowding through the enclosure, but discipline was strict, so, whatever they thought, they dared not stop.

"I hope the boats are all right," said Gillian. "Unlock the doors, Lulu, and let us see, since we *are* here."

Louise laughed. "With pleasure. I should like to see them as much as you," she said, selecting her key and going to the door. Her last speech was in French, of course, the next was English, for, as she reached the door, she uttered an exclamation of horror.

"What is wrong?" cried Paula, joining her.

The rest clustered round. Louise turned on them a face of utter disgust as she said, "Some filthy little wretch has been here and has literally *plastered* the door with chewing gum!"

It was true. Someone with misplaced energy had covered the door with long threads of chewing gum, and stuffed up the lock with the same viscous substance. The dark paint made the gum unnoticeable at a short distance, but whoever it was had done the work thoroughly – up to a point. The lower half of the door was covered. The upper half was clear, thus pointing directly to some child or children as the criminals.

"Dirty little *pigs*!" exclaimed Hilary. "Of all the disgusting things to do! What rotters some kids are!"

The rest were not far behind her in the matter of condemnation. Then Louise sent Arda flying for Miss Nalder, who, as games mistress, ought to know about it. She came, investigated, and expressed herself with a force that showed her annoyance.

"This means that one of the men must be taken from his work and set to scraping off this mess," she said wrathfully. "And it was all repainted during the holidays! I'd like to catch the young imps that did it. I'd teach them a lesson!"

The sound of the school bell sent them all flying for school, and they had to leave the mystery unsolved for the moment. Jockel, the boy-of-all-work, and not quite "all there", to quote Joey, was hauled forth from the shed where he was chopping wood, and set to cleaning the door.

69

Meanwhile, down in the bushes, two small people were hugging themselves with glee over the wrath of the Chalet School mistress and the Seniors.

"We'll do some more later," said Maria, when at last she rose from her cramped position and shook herself. "Come on, Mario. It must be time for collazione, and I'm hungry. Besides," she added prudently, "they may search these bushes, and if they found us, they would guess."

Mario agreed with this, so the pair, looking guilelessly sweet, left their hiding place and strolled round the lake to the hotel, there to make a good breakfast, chuckling to themselves at intervals over the success of their prank.

CHAPTER 6

Prefects' Meeting

"Joey! Oh, good! Come in and sit down."

The cry burst from Louise Redfield as she looked up on hearing the tap at the door, and saw it open, and Joey Bettany framed in the doorway.

Joey laughed and came forward, closing the door behind her. "What eager hospitality! Hello, everyone! We've come down for the next six or eight weeks. We're settled as far as we can be for the first evening, and, as Madge and Mamzelle were putting the babies to bed, and no one seemed to want me, I thought I'd stroll round here and see how you were all getting on."

"That's splendid. *We* want you! Come and sit down,

and give us your valuable advice."

"I'll give it to you. Whether it's valuable or not may be another matter." And Joey subsided into the big wicker chair Gillian pulled forward for her, and beamed at them. "Hello, Peri!" she added, as she caught sight of Hilary.

"Hello, Snowdrop's Prince! Been prostrating yourself before anyone lately?" came the instant retort.

Jo chuckled at this reminiscence of the sale the two schools had given during the Easter term of the previous year in aid of the free beds at the sanatorium, and then looked round. "You all look very worried. What's the matter?"

"Something no prefects ever had to meet before," replied Louise.

"What can that be? I had to face up to a good many odd things myself – Evvy and Co's jazz band among others, as you remember. What have those young things been doing now?"

"Oh, it isn't them," said Anne fervently, if ungrammatically. "As a matter of fact, Evvy and Co are most responsible people these days."

"What a strain for them!"

"Oh, come, Joey!" protested pretty Elsie Carr. "I can remember the time – not so very long ago, either – when you yourself were a nuisance to all prees. Don't talk as if you were an elderly party of ninety, for it won't work."

"I never was so bad as Evvy, and Corney, and that set," protested Jo.

"H'm! You never gave the school a horrid shock by going off after Elisaveta and that mad cousin who kidnapped her, did you?" demanded Margia Stevens. "*I* remember the shock we all had."

"That was long ago, in the dim and distant past— "

71

"Oh, stop talking about what happened in the Middle Ages, and turn your attention to the present!" cried Louise, tired of this exchange.

"Yes; what *has* been happening?" Jo suddenly produced a box of chocolate fudge, and handed it to the Head Girl. "Rally round that, everyone, and sample my last effort while you tell me your sad story."

"It began the first day we came back," began Louise, helping herself and handing the box to Anne.

"Yes; the snuff affair," agreed Hilary, who was at her other side.

"The snuff affair?" Jo wrinkled her brows. "What is all this?"

All talking together, they told her, and then passed on to the chewing gum mystery, as Margia insisted on calling it.

"Sounds like the latest thriller," said Jo.

"Oh dear, no!" said Gillian. "There was the affair of the frogs."

"The what? Look here, have you got mixed up with a detective omnibus book, or what?" demanded Joey.

"We've no idea. But a huge box came yesterday morning, by hand, for Mademoiselle Lachenais. She took it up to the staff room, as it came just before break, and she opened it up there. I don't know what she expected, but dozens of tiny frogs hopped out when she got it open," said Gillian.

"But how do *you* know what was in it, if it happened in the staff room," queried Jo.

"Bill had sent me up with our science notebooks, as her hands were full already," explained Gillian.

"But – where did it come from?"

"No one knows. At first they thought some of the

Middles had been doing it — I thought so myself," said Paula seriously. "Hilary says one or two of theirs are very mischievous; and you know yourself what some of ours are like— "

Jo interrupted her. "Why 'theirs' and 'our'? You're all one school now."

"No," said Arda unexpectedly. "We are in the same buildings, and we work and play together; but we are *not* one school yet. It is too soon."

Hilary nodded. "We're still inclined to think of ourselves as St Scholastika's, Jo. As Arda says, it's too soon for us to be really Chaletians. Of course, we like the school, and we're going to do our best for it. But we're Saints as well, still."

"I see. I suppose it *is* rather difficult," agreed Jo. "Well, go on with the frog story."

"Well, Mademoiselle gave a yell, and bounded onto the nearest chair; two or three other people yelled, too, and I nearly did myself. You've no idea what a shock it was. We caught the frogs, though, and put them into the fields, and that was that. The Abbess came in and saw it all, and she called the school together and talked very seriously about stupid practical jokes. She said that if anyone knew anything about it, they were to go to her in rest period. No one went, and the Middles and Juniors vow they know nothing about it. I believe them, too."

Jo sat silent for a few minutes. "Who brought the box?" she asked.

"Anna didn't know. She says it was a thin, very dark boy."

"With *curls* by any chance?"

The prefects stared at her. "How should we know?

73

We never asked. Margia, you're nearest the door. Run and ask Anna, will you?"

Margia went off, to return five minutes later with the information that Anna was sure that the boy had had straight hair.

"H'm!" said Joey.

"Joey, what do you know about it?" asked Louise curiously.

"Nothing, really; it was just an idea of mine."

"Yes; but what sort of an idea?" asked Anne.

"Honestly, Anne, I don't know anything about it. Is that all that's happened?"

"Up to date, yes. But three things like that happening, and nothing to account for them, is rather too much, I reckon," said Louise.

"I'm with you there. I wonder— " Jo went into a brown study, and the rest watched her curiously. They felt sure she knew something. Presently she looked up. "I'm afraid I can't help you – *yet*. And the only advice I can give you is to be on your guard."

"Someone seems to be at feud with us," said Hilary thoughtfully.

"No; it isn't with you – *as* you, I mean," replied Joey.

"Then what *do* you mean? Don't be so cryptic, Jo!"

"If it's what I think, then the little wretches have heard of Madge's connection with the school, and are doing these things to get back at her."

"What are you driving at? And don't use such slang! You'll corrupt our beautiful English if you talk like that," said Louise severely.

"You and your beautiful English!" But Jo decided to waste no further scorn on them. Instead, she told them of the first meeting with the Balbini twins, and

74

how Maria and Mario had vowed vengeance on them.

"And you think that these two have heard about Madame and are annoying us in the hope of annoying her?" queried Arda.

"Something like it."

"But what horrible children they must be!"

"Madge says they are more to be pitied than blamed," said Jo.

"Oh? Why is that?"

"Their mother is Princess Balbini, who is dying at the Sonnalpe," replied Jo soberly. "Their father is wrapped up in her, and doesn't bother about them. The aunt who is supposed to look after them can't control them in the least, and they seem to do as they like. I'm sorry about their mother, of course. From all accounts, they've never had much to do with her, as she's been ill ever since they were tiny. I suppose there *is* some excuse for them. But there's certainly no excuse for their messing up new paint with chewing gum – *or* trying to kill my sister with their wretched catapults!" she added wrathfully.

"I think there is a great deal of excuse for them," said Louise pitifully. "I heard about Princess Balbini when I was up with Leonard."

"That may be. But they're quite old enough to know there are things they can't do!"

"Well, this isn't doing much good," said Hilary impatiently. "How do you propose to deal with them – if it *is* them? If it were our own Juniors we could handle them easily. But what are you to do with two outsiders?"

"The best thing would be for them to come here," suggested Elsie Carr.

"Maria, perhaps. Mario's a boy, and we haven't a boys' section," Joey reminded her.

"School is, doubtless, the place for them," agreed Paula. "Could you not seek an interview with their father, Jo, and suggest it?"

"I can see myself! Besides, I don't believe he'd bother. I tell you, he's got only one idea – his wife. The twins come in at the tail end of everything as far as he's concerned. And I can't go trying to drum up pupils for my sister's school like that. She would never allow it," said Jo reasonably.

"But couldn't someone else do it?" asked Hilary. "Not that I'm anxious to add to our troubles," she added.

"Elizabeth Arnett and Betty Wynne-Davies are enough for any school. And then there's Alixe von Elsen and her crowd. If all this trouble is owing to that child – what d'ye call her? Maria? – and her brother, I shouldn't think they'd be peaceful members of any school."

"In any case," said Ida, suddenly joining in, "no one knows positively that they are responsible for all this. And I certainly don't see how they could climb up to the oriel window and chuck snuff about without being caught. I should say we'd better look nearer home. You can't go to their father with a whole lot of guesswork, you know; and you've nothing in the way of proof, have you?"

At this sensible view of the situation, which had struck no one else, they all looked crestfallen.

"Then what *are* we to do if it goes on?" demanded Louise.

"Be on your guard, as I said. And if I may suggest it, don't talk about it. You can't help things if it's those two, and talking won't get you anywhere," said Jo.

They gave up the riddle, and after hastily assuring Jo that her presence was most appreciated by them, proceeded to deal with ordinary school business, which was the real reason for the meeting.

Each girl had some special office appointed her, as well as those duties which the prefects shared. These were light, consisting mainly of taking preparation, seeing that rules were kept when the staff were not there, being responsible for games apparatus, and so on. Most of them had their jobs fixed already, since the custom of the school was to arrange them at the first meeting of the new school year, and not to alter them except for some grave reason. But Hilary was made assistant Games prefect; Ida undertook pets, since she was devoted to animals; Irene Silksworth became staff prefect, which meant seeing that the staff got their mid-morning milk safely; and Nancy Wilmot undertook to look after the Junior library.

"What about the magazine?" asked Joey.

"Oh, Stacie Benson is still editor, and, thank goodness, has another two years at least here; so that won't worry anyone for a while yet."

So it was decided, and the girls turned to the next thing – the half term holiday. Seven years before, when Madge Bettany, as she then was, had founded her school, she had arranged a treat for the girls to celebrate her birthday at their request. This treat had become a tradition in the school, and every summer term brought up the question, "What has Madame arranged for her birthday treat?"

"Do you know what is to happen this half term, Joey?" asked Anne.

Joey chuckled tantalizingly. "Don't I just! Wait till you hear! You'll all be dancing on your heads with excitement!"

"Joey! Don't be mean! Tell us, and stop giggling like a – a hyena!" cried Margia.

Joey looked aggravating. Then she suddenly changed her mind. "Well," she said slowly, obviously enjoying the suspense in which she was keeping them. "Madge thinks you all ought to know more about the Tyrol than you do. And, of course, I quite agree with her."

"Well? Go on!" said half a dozen voices as she paused here.

"We've discussed it very thoroughly," said naughty Jo, watching them squirm over her slowness. "And after a lot of consideration, Madge herself hit upon the idea."

"Joey Bettany! I'll come round and shake you if you don't go on!" declared Louise.

Jo raised her eyebrows. Then she relented. "Oh, all right! You're going to Salzburg for the weekend."

"Salzburg!" A perfect babel arose at this glorious news.

"Joey! How gorgeous! When will it be? Are you to come with us? Will Madame be there? Will— "

Jo clapped her hands for silence, and they hushed. "Now listen, and I'll tell you all I know. The babies, by the way, aren't included," she added in parenthesis. "They'll have their own trip. But all in St Clare's and Ste Thérèse's will go. You go by coach, and Rob and I are coming, too. We are going to Wanda von Echenau's – Wanda von Glück's, rather. I believe Paula and— "

But what more she would have said on the subject was doomed to be deferred to a later date, for at that moment, something round and dark shot through the open casement, and fell with a soft plop on the table. The next instant the girls were leaping to their feet, fumbling frantically for handkerchiefs, and holding their noses with exclamations of disgust. The thing had burst, and a most unpleasant stench was filling the room. Even as they made a rush for the door, there came an outcry from another part of the house, showing that others were afflicted in the same way.

"Stink bombs!" cried Joey, as she headed fugitives from the prefects' room. "Those little brutes are at it again!"

Half the girls had no idea what stink bombs might be; but the smell was overpowering and disagreeable. They poured out of doors, for more than the prefects' room had been invaded. Even the staff room had caught it, for one of the things had come through an open window and burst on Miss Nalder's table.

Jo made for the gate, followed by Anne, Louise, Gillian, and Hilary. But nothing was to be seen when they got there, save a few visitors who were strolling past, taking a promenade before dinner, and who looked amazed when the Chalet School gate was flung open and the angry girls streamed out.

Jo looked swiftly up and down the path through the gathering dusk of the early May evening; but there was no sign of the Balbini twins, so she had to turn back and lead the girls in again, her fury unsatisfied.

"But it *couldn't* have been them, Joey," Margia pointed out at Abendessen, to which Jo had accepted an eager invitation. "They simply couldn't have flung the things all that distance. Stink bombs are very light, and they wouldn't carry."

But Jo had got an idea. "No; I grant you they couldn't *throw* them. But they could fire them from air rifles. And *I* have cause to know that that boy Mario is a good shot."

"But Joey, there were stink bombs in many parts of the house," protested Paula. "How could they have managed that?"

"Easily," said Jo. "There are several other children at

that hotel. It would be a simple matter to round them all up into a gang. That child Maria has the wits to do it, too. That's what comes of taking children to the cinema!" she added.

"Well, it *may* be so; but again you've got no proof. It's only what you *think*," remarked Ida.

"Don't you worry. They've had success with their little jokes up to the present. If I'm any judge of character, that's going to make them careless, and they'll soon drop proof enough for anything about the place," said Jo calmly. "When that happens, I'm going to teach those babes a lesson they'll never forget. Rolls, please, Hilary!"

Well the Balbini twins *were* to have a lesson; but it was to be a far more terrible one than anything Jo ever could or would have devised; and, far from administering it, she was to do what she could to comfort the wicked pair through it.

CHAPTER 7

Dr Jem Encounters the Twins

Dr Russell was strolling along the path to Briesau where he was going to examine four people who had started suspicious spots. Not that Nurse feared much more than bilious rash; but in a school it is always advisable to take precautions. So Elizabeth Arnett, Kitty Burnett, Emmie Linders, and Biddy O'Ryan had been hustled into Isolation, and the four matrons had taken temperatures and examined tongues thoroughly that morning.

The doctor, a tall, fair man, with clean-cut face and a humorous mouth, was not thinking of anything in particular. Except for Princess Balbini, who was very ill, there were no critical cases at the Sonnalpe at present. His own family was flourishing, even the Robin, Primula Mary Venables, and little Peggy Bettany, the fragile members of it, being far stronger than they had been for some time. The move down to the lakeside appeared to be highly successful, and news from all relatives and friends was uniformly good. Therefore, having nothing to worry him for once, he was enjoying the fresh air of a lovely May morning, and the beauty of the flowers, the sparkling lake, the singing birds, and the bright sunshine.

Suddenly he was jolted out of his complacency by something that caught his hat and sent it flying. With an angry exclamation, he swung round, but the path behind him was bare; on one side was the lake and on the other the mountain wall which, just at this part, rose sheer for about fifteen feet. It must have been a piece of falling limestone, he supposed. He retrieved the hat from the hollow where it had fallen, pulled it down over his brows, and went on, resuming the cheerful whistle with which he had been enlivening his walk.

Smack! Something had flown past his face and struck the ground before him, rolling over the downward slope into the lake before he could catch it. Again he looked round, and again saw nothing. But this time he quickened his pace. If there was going to be a landslide of any kind just here, he must get to the phone and warn people to avoid the path for the present. Also, he must ring up an acquaintance of his, living in Spärtz, who was an authority on the subject of crustal movements of the earth, and get him to come up as soon as possible and investigate.

He reached the white-painted wooden paling that shut off the Briesau peninsula from the Seespitz path, passing through the gate, and turned to cross the rough pasture-land which spreads out just here. Again there came a slight thud and again his hat went flying.

This was beyond a joke, and Dr Jem, as the Chalet School people called him, realized that this was no effort of Nature's, but a deliberate onslaught by human agency. His wife had said nothing about her encounter with the Balbini twins, so he never suspected them. But he guessed that some small boy with a catapult was responsible for the trouble. Once more he swung round, and this time searched the landscape closely.

At first he saw nothing unusual – a couple of horses cropping the grass; two or three visitors strolling along by the side of the lake; an excited dog barking at its master, who was throwing sticks into the water for it. Then his eye was caught by the slight tremor of a low-growing bush near by. There was no wind to account for the movement, as it happened, and the angry man guessed that his persecutor was hidden there. He realized that he was too far away to catch anyone hidden behind it if he made a beeline for it, so he resorted to strategy. Picking up his hat, and ramming it once more onto his head, he resumed his walk, diverging slightly to his left, and thus bringing himself much nearer to the bush, yet so casually, that, to the observer, it must have looked merely accidental.

Phut! This time the missile struck him on the cheek. It was small, but it stung badly, and the doctor was throughly infuriated. With a sudden swift movement, he dived for the bush, and almost before his assailant had seen he was discovered, he found himself caught by the arm, hauled to his feet with scant regard for the thorns which clawed at him on the way, and dragged into the open by a big, very angry man.

Mario Balbini – almost unnecessary to name him – felt a shrinking down his spine as he looked up and encountered the glare of a pair of steely eyes. He felt that this time he had gone too far, and must pay for it. Then, for he was plucky enough, he set his teeth and stiffened himself to meet the payment.

"What do you mean by it, you young rascal?" demanded the doctor.

"I do not understand," said Mario in his own tongue. But if he expected to get away with that sort of thing, he found out his mistake very quickly.

"Indeed?" said the doctor, a certain deadly quiet in his tone. "Well, perhaps you will understand this instead." And, without more ado, he twisted Mario's head under his arm, and gave him such a sound, old-fashioned whipping as Master Mario had never had before in his life.

Blows were so new to him, that sheer astonishment kept the boy silent for the first two or three. Then, as the pain came home to him, he set up a scream like an hysterical steam-engine, and tried to kick the shins of his executioner. Dr Jem never turned a hair. He simply carried on till he felt that the young man had had a lesson he would remember. Then he released him, dropping him on the ground with a contemptuous, "There! Perhaps that will teach you to keep your impudent practical jokes to your own kind!"

Sobbing with the shock of the whipping, Mario raised a tear-stained face and glared at him. "I hate you – I hate you!" he gasped.

"Doubtless. But remember, you asked for your punishment. Now give me that catapult of yours – quick!"

"I won't! You shan't have it!" sobbed the boy defiantly.

Dr Jem put out a long arm, and lifted him to his feet. Mario cowered away from him – and could have kicked himself for doing so when he thought of it later on. But he need not have feared. Angry as he was, Dr Jem would never inflict cruel punishment on a child, and he knew that he had already given the little fellow as much as he ought to have at one time. He merely held him firmly while he plunged his hand into the numerous pockets – incidentally, getting his fingers unbearably sticky – until he found the catapult and a boxful of ammunition. These he shoved into one of his own pockets, and was about to release his captive when a man's gentle voice behind him said, "Good morning, Doctor. Has my small son been annoying you?"

The doctor turned round to face Prince Balbini, who had come along behind them in time to see and hear most of the business. Maria was with him, holding his hand. It was not often that he took notice of his children; but this morning his sister Emilia had succumbed to a sick headache, and he had undertaken to keep an eye on the pair. Emilia Balbini might be hopelessly incapable of managing the twins, but she did her best conscientiously; and, as Jo said, it would have puzzled an archangel to look after them properly all the time.

The sight of his father finished Mario's demoralization. He burst into tears again, and Maria tried to wrench her hand away from her father's to rush to his side. Vain effort! The prince merely tightened his hold on her with a sharp, "Be quiet, Maria!" and then repeated his question to the doctor.

"So it's your son, Prince?" said Dr Russell grimly.

"Yes; he has annoyed me, but he has paid up now, so we are all square, thank you."

Prince Balbini nodded. "Stop snivelling, Mario," he commanded in his gentle voice, which nevertheless held a certain steely inflexibility that seemed to have a good effect on the twins. Maria had ceased to wriggle, and Mario choked down his sobs and began to fumble for his handkerchief. The prince tossed his own to his small son and then turned to the doctor. "I apologize for Mario," he said. "As you have given him his punishment, we will say no more about it – this time." He eyed the black bruise on the doctor's cheek reflectively, and then went on: "I will relieve you of him now, Doctor. He can come with me." He stretched out his hand and took the boy by the shoulder. "Come, Mario; we looked for you before we left the hotel. If I had known how you were engaged—" He paused, and the little silence that followed was so full of horrid threats that Maria shivered.

"It was only a boy's nonsense," said the doctor, who had once more picked up his hat, which had fallen off in the struggle with Mario. "I won't ask him to shake hands with me now, he is feeling too sore, I expect" – a twinkle came into his eyes, but Mario, fuming over the double meaning of the speech, never saw it, and Maria would not – "but later on we shall make it up, I hope."

Prince Balbini smiled. "He will certainly be friends with you, Doctor. Mario owed you a debt; you have exacted payment, and he has paid, as a Balbini is always proud to do. That is the end of it. I appreciate your generosity and will permit him to accept it this time. Now we will continue our promenade."

Raising his hat, he turned and led the children back to the path, while the doctor made his way across the pasture to the side entrance of the school, and sauntered round the buildings to Isolation, where he inspected the patients, pronounced them to be suffering from no more than a tummy rash, shut himself up in the tiny dispensary attached where he concocted as evil-tasting a draught as ever the quartette had swallowed, found some lotion which turned the bruise on his cheek from black to yellow, and having attended to everything, sauntered home once more, chuckling to himself over the expressions of his latest patients when they had gulped down his mixture.

"And that will teach those four not to indulge in unripe gooseberries again in a hurry," he thought, as he reached the water meadows.

There came a sudden flash of white at this point, and he found himself suddenly confronted by a veritable little fury, in whom he recognized Maria di Balbini. He raised his hat to her with the grave courtesy he accorded to every small girl of his acquaintance – which may have been one reason for his popularity with the race.

But his courtesy availed him nothing on this occasion. Prince Balbini had taken his children as far as the Kronprinz Karl, the big hotel standing opposite the ferry landing, and then had turned round and walked them back to the Seehaus. Arrived there, he had sent Mario to make himself clean and tidy, bidden Maria take her book out to the verandah, and remember that she was not to leave the hotel grounds till he returned, and then got out his car and driven off to the Sonnalpe, where his wife was slowly slipping away from him, despite all the doctors could do for her.

He had spoken very sternly to the twins during their walk, assuring them that if he heard tales of any more such doings on their part as the assault on the doctor, he would send them away to school. As this would mean separation, he could have threatened nothing more awful to the pair. Not that they dreamed of giving up their foolish feud against Madge and her belongings; but they resolved to keep their doings more than ever secret from their father. But when he had gone, Maria had tossed down her book and flown upstairs to seek her brother and get from him the whole story of his encounter with the doctor.

Mario refused to say a word. He was lying on his bed, no cleaner than when his father had left him, and to all his sister's eager questioning he preserved a sullen silence. Despairing of getting anything out of him, she left the room, and at the door, ran into a thin sallow-faced boy about a year older than themselves. This was Manuel Madariaga, a small Spaniard with whom the twins had forgathered the previous week. The fact that his baptismal name began with the same letter as theirs had been a link between them. And then, Manuel had been in Spain during the early part of the reign of terror, and had hair-raising tales to tell them. He had been got out of the country as speedily as possible and really knew very little at first hand. But that meant nothing to the twins, who had thrilled to all he told them. His elder brothers were still in Spain; but his mother was up at the Sonnalpe, slowly recovering from all she had undergone, and from the shock of his father's death during an air raid. Manuel was down here with the aunt who had smuggled him out of Spain six weeks after the fighting began.

"Where's Mario?" demanded this young man of Maria.

"In there. He won't speak to me," she said. "Tell me, Manuel, what happened between him and the doctor?"

Manuel eyed her thoughtfully. "We went out with

our catapults," he said in his stumbling Italian. "We sat right up the mountainside – over there." He flung out his hand in a gesture that embraced the north and west of the lakeside, but she knew what he meant, and nodded.

"Yes? What then?"

"Why, that doctor who is the husband of the lady you hate came, and I crept further along to the big school. Mario knocked off his hat – it was a good shot," he added reflectively. "Then, as he came past, I aimed, but missed. So I ran through the brush right to the end, and took another shot at him, and sent his hat flying again. Dios! How angry he looked!" And he hugged himself with silent mirth.

"Never mind that!" said Maria impatiently. "What happened next?"

"Well, you see, Mario had gone past me, down to the meadows, and was hiding behind that big bush just at the entrance. The doctor began to cross the meadow, and Mario hit him on the cheek. But the doctor was ready – I cannot think why – and he rushed at the bush, and dragged poor Mario out, and beat him – hard!"

"Why did not you go to the rescue at once?" demanded Maria.

Manuel flushed darkly. "I could not. I was caught in a thorn bush, and by the time I got free it was all over, and you and your father were there, so I knew it was no use going. I came home, and Zia Dolores caught me, and scolded – oh, like a fishwife! She made me take off my clothes till she had mended them and I had to go to bed, for she would give me no others. And all the time she scolded and scolded. But the tears were bad ones – see!" And he turned his back to show the neatly mended rents, which certainly justified all Dona Dolores' lectures.

Maria nodded. "I see. It was not your fault, then. But – you say this – person – dared to beat the son of Prince Balbini?"

"Oh, yes; he beat him very hard, till Mario screamed," replied Manuel, piling on the agony.

Maria clenched her fists, and her great eyes flamed. "And my father knew – oh, yes; I see it now! That was why he spoke of payment! And he did *nothing*! And it was his *son* the brute had beaten!"

"Well, I expect he thought he had some excuse," said Manuel judiciously. "It was a bad bruise the doctor got."

But Maria refused to see it. "He shall pay – they shall all pay!" she hissed. "I go now to meet him and warn him, for never shall they say that a Balbini fell on them unawares. Go you, Manuel, and bid the Band meet us during the siesta hour near the syringas. There we will plan for revenge!"

Then she was off, to seek the unconscious doctor, and pour forth on him the full torrent of her wrath. She met him by the water meadows, by which time she had worked herself up into a full-paced rage. The doctor was startled by the child's appearance. He recognized her at once, and wondered what she wanted. He was left in no doubt; for, opening her mouth, she poured upon him such a stream of vituperation as fairly took his breath away for the moment. When he recovered it, he picked her up, struggling like a mad thing, and bore her to the lake-side.

"Now," he said sternly, "pull yourself together, or I'll put you into the water. Do you hear me? You'll be in hysterics next!"

Maria took no notice, so he heaved her up, as if to fulfil his threat, and she managed to control herself. Then he set her down, but still kept gentle hold of her. "Now what is it you want?" he asked quietly. "Tell me, and tell me calmly, or I'll carry you to the Seehaus, and tell your father you are to go to bed for the rest of the day."

Well aware that he was quite capable of doing it, and that, in that case, her father would obey him, Maria made an effort to speak coherently. "I am come to tell you that we hate you! You are a wicked, cruel man to beat Mario like that, and we will be revenged on you for it! You have roused the anger of the Mystic M," this with a sudden recollection of the last film she had seen, "and the Mystic M will make you pay!"

"I wonder what you've been seeing at the cinema lately?" said the doctor imperturbably. "For pity's sake, child, talk like a Christian! You aren't a movie star, and there's no need to be ill-bred, no matter how angry you are. Vulgarity won't help you, you know."

Brought up short like this, Maria opened and shut her mouth once or twice like a gaping fish. Not thus was she accustomed to being treated in her all too frequent fits of passion. Zia Emilia wept, and wrung her hands impotently. Old Detta, their nurse, cried on all the saints in heaven to help expel the demon that had taken possession of her darling (contrary to tradition Detta preferred Maria to her brother) and lit endless candles with that end in view. But this quiet, rather contemptuous treatment was something new.

Seeing that he had taken the wind out of her sails, the doctor proceeded (as he hoped) to settle her finally. "Mario deserved all he got. It's time someone showed you two that you don't own the earth. There are other people in it, and you have to learn to live with them. That's one reason why we're sent into the world. That's one reason why I gave Mario his thrashing. Try to understand, Maria. You aren't a baby, you know. You can reason things out for yourself. If everyone tried to behave as you and Mario do, a nice world this would be! And you've no more right to it than anyone else; remember that! And here's another thing. *You* won't be blamed for your bad conduct half as much as your father and mother, and the rest of the family. You're proud of being a Balbini, aren't you? Well, you're bringing disgrace to your name by your behaviour. Now run along; and think over what I've said to you, won't you? Goodbye – or, as you say, addio!" He released her, raised his hat to her, and walked away with all flags flying.

Maria turned round and watched him, her mouth still open, her eyes wide. When she had recovered from the shock of being talked to like that, she turned and went slowly back to the hotel, inwardly vowing that she would never think again of what the doctor had said to her. And never, NEVER would she forgive him till she had avenged her brother's wrongs!

Unfortunately for the first part of her resolve, she found that our minds are not so easily controlled as all that. Despite herself, she caught herself remembering what the doctor had said at odd intervals, and not only remembering, but meditating on it – all of which, when you came to think of it, was thoroughly aggravating.

CHAPTER 8

The Feud Progresses

For the next week things went peacefully. Whatever
decision the Mystic M had come to, its members did
nothing of any importance, such minor affairs as a heavy
letter, unstamped, arriving for Jo Bettany, and proving to
contain nothing but a sheet of brown paper folded small,
and a sudden storm of unripe gooseberries flung over the
garden palings among the babies while they were playing
happily, not being worth counting. Joey paid the double
postage, and execrated the sender of the "letter" with
all the force of her vocabulary; and Rosa the nurse and
Mamzelle dried the little ones' tears, and soon made them
happy again.

On several occasions Jo, walking round to the school,
met the Balbini twins, generally with three or four other
children from the Seehaus. They made faces at her, and
she grimaced back with a will, beating them at their own
game every time. It was undignified, and she took good
care not to let the Russells hear of it, but it relieved her
feelings.

At school, the aliens were beginning to settle down;
and the younger girls, at least, were beginning to feel
complete Chaletians. The older ones naturally took longer
over it.

"There are those kids from the new hotel," said
Cornelia Flower at break one pouring wet day.

The girls had got up to find the windows obscured by a veil of silver rain, and there would be no going out that day for them unless it cleared up later, which it showed no signs of doing. The Seniors were all in their common room, drinking milk, and eating bread twists. The two Fifths had science the last half of the morning, and Miss Wilson had sent word that they might take their lunch to the lecture room and eat it there to save time. The Middles were over at St Clare's, the two Fourths having been there for geography and art, while the Thirds had been sent across as they were due for domestic science. The Juniors, of course, were at their own house.

At Cornelia's words, two or three of the girls turned.

"Not out in all this rain, surely, Corney?" said Hilary, rather horrified. "What on earth can their people be thinking about to allow it? They'll get their deaths of cold!"

"Not they! Kids like that are born to be hanged!" vowed Evadne.

"What are they doing?" asked Paula, coming over to see.

"Just wandering round the fence – and much good may it do them!" said Cornelia viciously.

But Louise looked troubled. "I don't know about the others; but I surely reckon those Balbini children ought not to be out there. Their mother is dying at the Sonnalpe of TB. Kids like that oughtn't to be allowed to take such risks."

"You can bet your bottom dollar their folks don't know where they are," declared Cornelia. "Say, someone, oughtn't we to let the Abbess know? Guess she'd be able to deal with them all right."

"She's right," said Hilary. "Louise, suppose you go

93

and tell the Abbess? If their mother's so ill, I'm certain those twins oughtn't to be prancing about in this. Why, the rain's coming down in cartloads!"

Louise agreed, and went off to the study to seek Miss Annersley, who looked distressed when she heard the news. "Those poor children ought certainly not to be out in such a downpour. Thank you, Louise. I'll see about it."

Louise took the hint and withdrew, and the Head turned to Miss Stewart, who had been chatting with her and sharing her coffee.

"Best send Nell Wilson out to them," said that young lady. "From all I've heard, it needs someone like a sergeant-major to impress those imps."

"Well, go and tell her, then," said the Head, turning to the switchboard of the telephone. "I'll ring up the Seehaus, meanwhile, and see if I can get on to any of their people."

"Right! I'll see to it. Shall I ask Maria for hot milk as I go past the kitchen?"

"Yes; that's a good idea, Con. And tell her to send some bread twists too."

Miss Stewart nodded, and went off cheerfully, while Miss Annersley speedily got on to the Seehaus hotel, contrived to find someone who would come round for the children, and then turned to clear chairs and window seats of papers and books in readiness for her unexpected guests.

Meanwhile, Miss Wilson had flung a raincloak over her head and gone to summon the enemy to the school. Rather to her surprise, they came at once, and meekly followed her into the Chalet, and along the corridor to the pleasant study, where a bright fire was glowing in the stove, since it was a cold as well as a wet day, and two of the maids were bringing in jugs of steaming milk and baskets of bread twists, as well as big mugs.

At this, the party looked rather taken aback. Still, Mario advanced to the tall Miss Annersley with his most seraphic smile, and said politely, "Thank you, Signorina. We had thought the rain would stop, but it only became worse."

"You ought never to have come out in such rain," said Miss Annersley. "You are terribly wet. Take off your caps and coats, and sit down. You must all have some of this hot milk, or you'll be taking a fine crop of colds back to the Seehaus."

They meekly shed their outer raiment, and sat down in silence. Miss Annersley looked at them, and smiled. "Suppose you tell us your names? At present, I know only Maria and Mario Balbini. What are the rest of you called?"

Silence, during which the party looked at each other. Finally, Mario came to the rescue. "Perhaps I had better explain," he said, in the clear, fluent English which was a legacy from the time when he and Maria had had an English nursery governess. She had lasted only ten months. At the end of that time she had resigned her well-paid post, vowing that she would sooner teach Hottentots than the Balbini twins. But during her reign, she had managed to teach the pair English, and their father had seen that they kept it up, because, though they knew nothing about it at present, he fully intended both to go to school in England.

Miss Annersley smiled at him. "Perhaps it would be best," she agreed.

So he began. "These are Myfanwy and Morwenna Davies," he said, indicating two fair-haired girls of about his own age. "This is Manuel Madariaga. This girl is Mélanie Kerdec; and this boy is Murdoch Macintosh."

Miss Annersley looked startled. "All Ms!" she said. "What a coincidence!"

At her words, Mélanie giggled, but stopped when she received a warning glance from Maria.

"It *iss* strange," said Morwenna, the elder of the two Davies girls. "*We* thought that."

"But it iss nice, too," added Myfanwy, equally Welshly.

"So you two are true Welsh?" said Miss Wilson abruptly. "And Mélanie is Breton, of course."

"And Aa'm Scotch," put in Murdoch, whose hair of fiery red made him noticeable among the black or flaxen heads of the rest. "Aa'm frae Glesgie, ye ken."

"I daresay," said Miss Wilson drily. "Still, there's no need to adopt the brogue to tell us that." Whereat Murdoch went scarlet under the liberal crop of freckles that adorned his face.

"Manuel is Spanish," said Maria suddenly. "He has been through the Spanish Terror, and can tell us of terrible things."

Miss Annersley smiled. "I met your mother, Manuel, last Sunday when I was up at the Sonnalpe. She told me about you."

Manuel promptly rivalled Murdoch's blushes, and the conversation languished.

The Balbini twins looked at each other. They had planned this visit, of course. They had their own reasons for getting into the Chalet. But so far, nothing had gone just as they had intended. Maria decided that something must be done about it. With a smile as seraphic as her brother's, she asked prettily, "Oh, Signorina, now that we are here, may we ask you to show us your school? We hear so much about it at the hotel. It would be pleasant to see it."

"I'm afraid we can't show you much," said Miss Annersley. "The girls are at lessons, you see, so the form rooms are all in use."

"But even a little," pleaded Maria. "It would be something to talk about."

Miss Annersley gave her a speculative look. She had heard something – not much, though – about Joey's and Mrs Russell's first encounter with these children, and this sudden interest in the school looked rather suspicious to her. Then she looked at the child again. Maria was the picture of innocence as she stood there, her vivid little face uplifted in pleading, her glorious eyes full of wistfulness. The Head knew what was coming to the Balbinis. She suddenly felt sorry for them. After all, it could do no harm to show them two or three of the rooms. One or two classrooms were vacant; and they could see Hall and the library. Perhaps Miss Wilson would permit a peep at her precious laboratories.

"We can't show you much," she said, rising. "However, we will do what we can. Drink up your milk, and then we will go. I expect someone will be coming to take you home presently."

The children looked uncertainly at the mugs of steaming milk they all held. However, something in the steady eyes on them made them meekly drink up the milk. But with one accord they declined the bread twists. Seeing that they meant what they said, she let it go, and escorted them out of her study, and over the bottom floor of the school, while Miss Wilson departed to her own kingdom.

They saw two classrooms and Hall, and then were taken upstairs to look at the library. The Davies pair looked wistfully at the cases containing story books, but said nothing. Miss Annersley wondered if the girls would consider lending these children a few of their books. It was unlikely that they had much literature with them, and children's books were not likely to be found in a hotel. However, she could say nothing till the girls were consulted, so, when they had gazed their fill, she led the visitors out.

"And a sleep room – a dormitory, is it not?" pleaded Maria. "We should so like to see one."

Miss Annersley laughed. "They are quite ordinary bedrooms, Maria. Only they have several beds in them, and the beds are divided from each other with curtains. I'm afraid they're not very interesting."

"They are awfully interesting to us," said Morwenna. "We haff neffer been to school, but we haff read about them, and it would be so nice to see a real dormitory."

"Poor bairns!" thought the kind-hearted Head. "I expect they find hotel life very dull in this kind of weather." Then she addressed them: "Well, perhaps I might show you one, as one is fairly near. Come along, and you shall see Green."

But the boys hung back. "Please, Signorina, we are not so interested as the girls. May we not await you in the hall?" asked Mario.

"Oh, we won't keep you a minute," began Miss Annersley.

"But we would be very good. We would sit on that big seat you have there, and not wander about," he said seriously.

"Aa don't think it's juist right for laddies to be keeking at young leddies' rooms," said that red-headed Scot Murdoch, unexpectedly.

Miss Annersley gasped. Then, seeing that the boys meant what they said, and thinking the quickest way would be to let them do as they suggested, she agreed. "Oh, very well, then. But you must promise me not to go further than the hall. Lessons are going on, you see, and we can't have you wandering into form rooms and startling the girls."

"We will go no further than the hall," promised Mario quickly.

So she gave way, and while she escorted the four little girls down a passage to view Green, the boys went gravely downstairs to the big square hall, with its plants, and old settle, and comfortable chairs. Later on, Miss Annersley could have kicked herself for being taken in so easily. But just at the time, she was thinking more of the fact that in ten minutes' time she was due with the Upper Sixth, and hoping that whoever came for the children would not delay much beyond that time.

She showed the girls the dormitory, and when they had exclaimed over all the dainty arrangements to their hearts' content, led them downstairs to the hall, where they found the three boys sitting together on the old settle, looking as grave as judges.

By this time, the little Davies' clergyman brother had arrived with a big car to take the septet home, so they got into raincoats and caps, said goodbye affably, and went off with David Davies, who was not unnaturally annoyed at having to turn out in such weather, and told his little sisters what he thought of them in no uncertain terms.

The sequel came at half-past nineteen that night. The heavy clouds still hung low, and the valley, overshadowed by the towering lines of the limestone crags, was dusky by that time. Margia, requested by Louise to switch on the lights in the prefects' room, switched in vain. So did sundry other people, though from St Clare's, St Agnes, and St Hild's, as the staff hostel was now called, lights were twinkling forth.

"Something must have fused, or there's been a blow-out," said Margia at last. "Well, it's only dusk yet, mercifully. Shall I go to the Abbess about it, Lulu? It may be the bulb, and she could give us a fresh one."

"Funny thing if *four* bulbs all went off at once," said Hilary suspiciously.

"Oh, it can happen, I guess," said Evadne Lannis cheerfully.

"Yes; you'd better go," agreed Louise. "*Some*thing must have happened to the thing."

Margia opened the door, and found the corridor in darkness. "I say, it looks as if it must be a fuse! The lights have gone all over."

"Then it's something wrong at the main," said Evadne, wagging her head till the fair curls she wore tied in a bunch at her neck bobbed wildly.

At this moment a light showed along the corridor, and Miss Annersley was among them. "What are you doing here, girls? Go back to your room at once. Yes; I know there's something wrong with the lights, but that is no reason why prefects should set the rest of the school a bad example. Miss Wilson will be along presently, and will see what is wrong. Meantime, go back and wait till the lights come on."

Reluctantly they obeyed her, and sat down in their places once more.

"If I didn't know it was impossible, I'd say that crew

100

that were hanging round here this morning had had something to do with it," grumbled Margia. "I ought to be at the piano now, anyway, but how can I practise in the dark like this? And Herr Anserl will bite my head off tomorrow if I don't know my Bach." And Margia, who was destined to be a concert performer, heaved a gusty sigh.

"The Abbess will give you extra time," said Evadne consolingly as she tilted her chair backwards.

Tilting was forbidden, since Margia's small sister, Amy, had once had a nasty fall through doing it. Evadne was a bad sinner in this direction, and now retribution came upon her as she raised the front legs of her chair, and balanced it back at a dangerous angle. The chair had been subjected to some years of hard treatment, and this was the final straw. The back legs parted company with the rest of it, and Evadne landed on the floor with a crash which startled the girls and jarred her unpleasantly.

There was a rush to pick her up, of course, and in the now fast gathering darkness, one of the girls trod on her hand, while someone else kicked her knee. She let out a howl which made them draw back in real alarm, and brought from Louise a startled exclamation of, "Evvy! Are you hurt?"

"Hurt? Of course I'm hurt! Guess you'd be hurt, too, if you'd sat down with a bang, and then some idiot tried to make a doormat of you while some other idiot took you for a football!" retorted Evadne. "Hurt! You bet I'm hurt!"

"It is so dark to see," apologized Paula. "Can you get up, Evvy?"

"Of course I can! D'you think I'm paralysed?" And Evadne rose from the floor in a bad temper. She sat

101

down in the nearest seat with an involuntary "Ow!" since she was badly bruised, and the girls awaited events in silence.

Nothing happened. They had been nearly ten minutes in the dark now, and it began to look suspiciously as though something really bad had happened to the light, when they heard footsteps, and pretty Miss Stewart came into the room, carrying a torch in each hand.

"Miss Stewart; what *is* the matter with the light?" cried Anne, as Louise, who was nearest Evadne, bent to inspect her anxiously.

"Matter?" Miss Stewart had a peppery temper, and it was clear that she was annoyed. "Why, someone has taken all the fuses out of the fuse box, and cut some wire or other. Miss Wilson has put in new fuses, but the light is still out, so it is plain that it is more than that. Do you girls know if any of the Middles or Juniors have been playing tricks?"

"No; I'm sure they haven't," said Gillian. "For one thing, I don't believe any of us know where the fuse box is. *I* don't!"

"It's in that cupboard under the stairs," said Miss Stewart.

"Then I'm sure no one knew. I always had an idea it was in the cupboard next door to the stockroom – what used to be stationery," said Louise, looking up from Evadne.

"Well it's a great nuisance. What I came to say was that someone will be here shortly with candles for you, but Miss Annersley says you must not try your eyes with working by them. You are to put your books away, and go to the common room and dance until the light is put right. – Well, Margia? What is wrong with *you*?" For Margia had uttered an unearthly groan.

"My practice, Miss Stewart! I've a new Bach for Herr Anserl, and it still needs heaps of work. Oh, *wouldn't* I like to wring whoever's neck it was that did it!" And Margia stamped her foot with vexation.

"That will do. Don't give way to childish tantrums," said Miss Stewart coldly. "You can quite well go to practise at St Clare's. Run along, and ask whoever is on duty which music room is free. – Ah! Here come the candles!" as Maria from the kitchens arrived with two satellites, bearing trays of candles.

The girls hailed their arrival with relief, and, once the maids had departed to other regions, and Miss Stewart had also gone, they gathered their books together, and put them away, while Margia went to seek her music and then a piano where she could practise to her heart's content.

"You'll have to go to Miss Annersley about that chair, Evvy," said Louise. "And don't you think you ought to see Matey about the knock you had? It was a nasty blow, and you may have hurt yourself badly."

"Go to Matey! What d'you take me for?" demanded Evadne. "They'll be mad enough about the lights and the chair. I'm not shoving my head into any den of lions, I guess! Don't you worry, Lulu; I'll be all right after a night in bed. Guess I won't dance, though. I shan't mind a mite. I'm tired, and I'm stiff."

"But the chair?" urged Louise,

"I'll tell the Abbess in the morning. I'm saying nothing tonight." And from this decision she refused to budge.

The Sixth gave it up as a bad job, and went to dance. Evadne followed, but only to lie down on a settee and try to fight the bad headache which her fall had brought on. No lights but candles were available that night, for Miss

Wilson found that, in addition to removing the plugs, the criminal, whoever he was, had stuck a knife into the entrails of the fuse box, and it would require an electrician to right matters.

Of course, when it was all over, everyone guessed what had happened. Those boys, left to themselves, had found out where the box was, and done the mischief. Later still, they learned that Mario had got the information from the feeble-minded Jockel, and the whole thing had been planned.

"It takes a boy to think of such a thing," said Miss Annersley as she dialled the Seehaus number. "Trust a boy to contrive it! Well, I only hope that my report will result in something that will make those little wretches sit up! That's all!"

CHAPTER 9

The Prince Intervenes

If the feud did nothing else, it had one good effect. It brought the two parties in the Chalet School together. As Arda had told Jo, they were still, to a great extent, two parties. The Juniors were less divided, naturally; but as you went up the school, you found that St Scholastika's and the Chalet were still unwelded. This attack on the school helped to unite them.

"I think it's the limit!" pronounced Hilary next morning during break, when they were all out of doors. The rain had ceased overnight, and the morning had broken hot and sunny, with the thermometer rising rapidly. It had seemed good to the authorities to ordain an extra-long break as a result. The girls had been closely confined to the house for the past few days, and fresh air was desirable for them. Too many of them were connected with the heavy shadow of the Sonnalpe for those in charge to do other than set health first of all. Education came very much second in such matters.

"It's such a stupid situation," agreed Louise. "We can't do a thing about it, for they aren't ours. All we can do is stand by and keep a stiff upper lip while those little nuisances rag us. It's outrageous!"

"Don't worry," said Elsie Carr soothingly. "The Abbess is furious about the lights. I happen to know that she phoned a pretty stiff message to Prince Balbini last night. He's bound to take some notice."

Gillian, who had spent the weekend at the Sonnalpe, looked up with gravity in her pansy-blue eyes. "Princess Balbini is dying," she said slowly. "Dr Jack told me so last Sunday. They don't think she will live out the week."

"Oh!" The young faces grew serious. Elsie's only sister had been very ill when she came out three years before, though now she was practically cured. Louise's little brother would never be able to live away from the mountains. Several of the others had relations up there for treatment. The girls could sympathize with even the wild twins who had wrought such mischief.

"Do they know?" asked Louise.

"I don't think so," said Elsie. "Jo says that their father thinks them too young."

"Poor little souls!" said Anne pityingly.

Gillian glanced at her. "I feel as if the prince may not bother, even over the Abbess's message. He's up there nearly all the time, you know. The princess wants him, Dr Jack says."

"Well, he's not there now," said Evadne, glancing across the pergolas. "Here he comes, and those twins with him."

"Don't look!" said Louise quickly. "Let's go round and see what the others are doing."

The girls trooped off through the garden, and joined the rest; so Prince Balbini and his children made their way to the house, not realizing that they had been seen.

Anna answered the door, and ushered them into the study where Miss Annersley was sitting glancing over a letter which had come that morning from Mademoiselle Lepâttre. She lifted her head as the maid announced the visitors. Then she stood up, and her pleasant face was very grave.

The prince came in, bowing to her, Maria and Mario behind him, both looking sulky, though at a word from their father, Maria cutseyed, and Mario bowed to the lady.

"Buon giorno, Signorina," said the prince. "I have brought my children that they may apologize to you for all the trouble they and their friends have caused. Children!"

At the word, the twins advanced three steps, and stood with their long lashes cast down. Speaking together, "I beg your pardon most humbly, Signorina," they said, with nothing particularly humble in either voices or looks.

"Is that all you have to say?" said their father sternly.

"I promise not to do such a thing again," they repeated, very unwillingly.

Miss Annersley smiled. "Then we will say no more about it," she said quietly.

"You are most kind, Signorina." The prince glanced

106

at the children. "I am afraid my children have utterly disgraced me and the family. I have punished them severely for it, and I trust you will permit that they make good the damage they have done."

Miss Annersley bowed. She quite agreed with him that the pair ought to pay for the mischief they had wrought. Then she realized that the prince was looking at her pleadingly, and wondered what he wanted.

"I am separating them," he said slowly. "It is time Mario went to school, and it has long been arranged that he goes to Beaumont College in England. I have a deep admiration for the English education."

The Head glanced at the children, and saw Maria's face twitch convulsively, while Mario's lips were set in a straight line, and he was digging his toe in to the rug.

"I am sorry it should mean this," she said slowly. "Twinship is such a very close tie."

"Signorina, I know that. Unfortunately, the tie between my children is not for good. That is only too plain. However, we must remedy that." Then he looked straight at her. "I wonder if I might beg a few minutes with you in private?"

"Certainly," she said courteously. "I will send for my senior mistress, Miss Wilson, who is free at this time, and she will take charge of the twins while we have our talk." As she spoke, she rang the bell and presently Miss Wilson appeared, and after a few words of explanation from the Head, went off, towing the reluctant twins after her.

But when the children had gone, Prince Balbini seemed in no haste to begin his confidence. Miss Annersley sat back in her chair, and looked at him. Clearly, she must be the one to start the conversation.

"What is it you want to say to me?" she asked gently.

"Signorina," he said slowly, "I think you will know – what awaits us up at the Sonnalpe? My – my wife— "

"I know." Miss Annersley said no more. She guessed that this stern-faced man found it hard to talk of his adored wife who was dying.

"Then you will probably realize that, owing to her illness, my children have not had the guardianship they should have had. My sister is a good woman, and loves them dearly; but they are wilful and headstrong – true Balbinis there, I am afraid – and they are beyond her control. I am to blame, of course. I should have seen it. But I have had much else to trouble me, and indeed I had no idea of the lengths to which they could go. Then I met Dr Russell the other day, having an encounter with Mario, whom he had whipped – deservedly. Mario had had his fun and he paid only what was fair. I warned both of them at the time that if I had any further complaints about them, I should separate them. I thought the threat would have been sufficient; but it was not. I must apologize for the inconvenience you have suffered yesterday. Mario I have whipped again, and I have told him that I am sending him to school in England as soon as the authorities will have him."

"But," began Miss Annersley, "I scarcely think Beaumont will take him. He is too young, I feel sure. He would have to go to a preparatory school."

The prince made an impatient gesture. "All one! He goes to England. I like the English education, and I think Mario needs the kind of training he would get there more than most boys. There remains Maria. I do not intend that she shall go to England, though I am anxious that she, too, should have an English training. My wife was educated at an English convent, and was very happy there. But if

108

they are in the same country, I feel sure they will try to meet."

He paused, and looked at her. Miss Annersley was silent. She guessed where all this talk was tending, and she had not the slightest wish to receive Maria Balbini at the Chalet School. At the same time, she felt very sorry for this man whose heart was plainly breaking over his wife, and who must yet leave her at this time to deal with his rebellious children.

"Will you not help me, Signorina?" he asked. "Will you not receive the child as a pupil here? I will engage that she shall behave herself."

"Prince Balbini," said Miss Annersley abruptly, "why do you not tell the children about their mother?"

He made a gesture. "Signorina, they are so young. I do not wish to shadow their lives so soon."

"And yet," said Miss Annersley quietly, "the shadow is falling nearer and nearer every day. Would it not be kinder to warn them? Are you not afraid of the shock it will be to them when it comes?"

He looked perplexed. "That is true. But— "

"Forgive me!" Miss Annersley spoke impulsively. "Perhaps I have no right to speak, but I do think they should have some preparation. Your little Maria will need her mother presently, Prince. In a very few years she will be old enough to resent your having kept her in the dark. Believe me, I know. I speak from experience. I became a motherless child when I was thirteen. My mother was dying for weeks beforehand, and I was told nothing till my eldest brother came to my school to bring me home because my mother was dead. The knowledge that I might have been spared the terrible shock if I had only known that she was so ill embittered all my early girlhood. Oh, save your little Maria from a similar experience! Tell her and her brother that their mother is going from them very soon, and let them have *some* preparation."

"Perhaps you are right," he said. "I will consult my sister, and see what she says. And now, Signorina, will you consider my request and permit me to send Maria here – next week, if possible?"

Miss Annersley shook her head. "I'm afraid I can't do it this term," she said. "We are full up, and have no room at all. But some of our older girls are leaving at the end of this term, and we are also building a new house which should be ready in September. If you care to send Maria to us next term, Prince, I will take her then. But I can't take anyone this term. You see, we are over-crowded as it is." And she went on to explain to him about the joining up of St Scholastika's with the Chalet.

"I see," he said. "You could not take her, of course. But next term I may hope you will accept her?"

"Next term, with pleasure. She will understand, of course, that she must submit to discipline. If she did not, I must send her away, and that is a disgrace I would not willingly inflict on any child."

His eyes flashed. "It is a disgrace I could not bear to think would happen to her. I will talk to her very seriously, and see that she quite understands what insubordination would mean for her."

"And as for Mario," went on the kindly Head, "I am afraid you will have the same difficulty there. We are nearly at the end of May. Most schools would prefer to take a new pupil at the beginning of term. I doubt if any school would have him at this date."

"I must get someone to take charge of them," he said heavily. "I – I cannot spare the time – *now*."

110

"That I quite understand. And tell them the news of their mother's very serious illness. I am sure if they understood they would not indulge in such wild pranks."

"I will discuss it with my sister," he promised. "If she agrees, they shall be told that their mother is – is— "

"I am sure you would be wise to do so," said Miss Annersley.

"Very well," he said, rising. "And now, I must not interrupt you any longer. If you will send for the children, we will take our leave."

Miss Annersley complied, and while Anna went off to seek the children, the prince turned again to her.

"Letters from them to your girls will arrive today, to apologize for their bad behaviour, Signorina."

Miss Annersley smiled. "I am not so sure that *all* my girls objected to the episode, Prince. Do you think it necessary?"

"Yes," he said curtly. "If for no other reason, because they stand in much need of humility. I hope this will be a lesson to them."

Miss Annersley could say no more; and then Miss Wilson arrived, bringing the sulky pair with her. Their father bade them thank the lady for so kindly looking after them, and they mumbled something that might pass for thanks. He sighed, and then waved them to the Head.

"Bid the Signorina buon giorno, children."

The pair darted furious looks at Miss Annersley, but obviously they stood in some awe of their father, and did as he bade them. Then he took them off, and the Head and her friend were left to discuss the affair alone.

"You advised him very wisely, Hilda," said Miss Wilson before she departed once more.

"I hope so," sighed Miss Annersley. "But oh, to have

such a firebrand as Maria Balbini in the school next term!"

"We've had firebrands before," said her friend consolingly. "Anyhow, it isn't till next term. You bother yourself with what's going to happen this, and don't meet trouble halfway. Now I must run! Four B are due for science! Auf wiedersehn till Mittagessen!"

CHAPTER 10

Sybil Disappears

"Joey!"

"Yes?"

"You might go and bring Baby and Jackie in for their midday nap. It's too hot for them to take it outside today. I told Rosa they were to come in at eleven, and here it is half-past, and they're still out there!" Madge Russell sounded ruffled, and small wonder! The thermometer was at 86 degrees in the shade, and the sun was blazing down.

With a groan, Jo pulled from her typewriter the sheet she had just finished typing, tossed it down on a pile of others, and got up.

"How are you getting on?" asked her sister curiously. "You've been at that book since April, and I've not seen a line yet."

"Oh, it's coming," said Jo from the doorway. "You can take the first two chapters or so if you like."

"Very well. I'll glance at them while you fetch the babies." And as Jo vanished, Madge picked up the typed sheets, and settled down to await the arrival of her small daughter and nephew. Jo would not hurry; it was too hot, and the children's play place was at the far end of the garden, under the trees. She would have time to read a chapter.

The story described the adventures of a fourteen-year-old girl in the Tyrol, and was written in Jo's racy, graphic style. Madge lost herself in the first chapter. She read on, and finished the second. Then she suddenly realized that Jo had had time to get to the garden and back twice over, and still had not returned. What in the world was she doing?

The telephone bell rang, and Madge laid down her sheets and went to answer it. It was her husband, speaking urgently. "That you, Madge? Look here! Princess Balbini has rallied a little and is asking for the children, but no one at the hotel seems to know anything about them. Will you send Jo and Rosalie to look for them – they can't be far."

"Of course! Oh, Jem, is there the least chance, do you think?"

"Not a chance, I'm afraid. Both lungs are practically gone, and this rally is the final flicker. That's why I don't want any time wasted. If she goes back, the end will be quick. Hurry Jo and Rosalie!"

"I'll send them at once!" Madge rang off, and hurried out of the room to seek her sister and her husband's private secretary. She went to the office first, and told Rosalie what was wanted. Rosalie, a fair, very quiet girl, and an old Chaletian, jumped up at once.

"I'll go without waiting for Jo, Madame. Tell her I'll take the Seespitz end, and she can hunt down to Maurach. And wouldn't it be as well to ring up the school? They may have seen those poor children somewhere, and Miss

Annersley would send someone to find them and bring them along."

"Good idea! I'll ring them up, and you get off. Jo went to bring Sybil and Jack in from the garden, so she'll be here by the time I've told Miss Annersley."

Rosalie nodded. Just as she reached the front door, she turned back. "What shall I tell them if I find them, Madame? They don't know, do they?"

"No; their father meant to tell them, and then the princess was suddenly worse, and he was phoned for, and I don't suppose he ever thought of it again. Just tell them their mother wants them, and we have a car here, ready to take them up."

Rosalie raced off after that, despite the heat; and Madge, at the telephone, saw through the open door that she was running down the path to the water meadows.

Miss Annersley, rung up in the middle of a lesson, was deeply sympathetic, and promised to send out people to look for the missing pair. She also promised to have the school car standing ready to run them to St Scholastika's if they turned up. Then she rang off, and Madge turned back to the girls' study, to send Jo off in short order.

No Jo was there, but the Robin had come in from the front garden where she had been curled up in the hammock, reading.

"Has Jo been in?" asked Madge.

"No, Tante Guito. I haven't seen her," replied the small girl.

"Oh? Then I expect she took the babies straight upstairs to the night nursery. All right, Rob; I'll go up there and see her." Madge nodded to Robin, and went down the corridor and upstairs to the big, airy room which was the night nursery. It was empty. The shutters had been

114

closed, and it was comparatively cool and shady; but no babies lay in the cots.

"How annoying of Jo!" exclaimed the elder sister. "She must be stopping to play with the children, I do think that when I send her on an errand she might do it and not loiter! I shall speak to her about this."

She left the room, and made her way downstairs. Just as she reached the front door, there was the sound of flying footsteps, and then Jo, her face white, her eyes frightened, came tearing in.

"What is the matter?" demanded Madge. "Where are Baby and Jackie? What have you been doing?"

Jo took no notice of the sharpness of her tone. "Madge! Baby's missing!" she gasped. "We can't find her anywhere!"

"Nonsense! What are you talking about? *Missing?* How could she be missing?"

Jo collapsed into the nearest chair, panting. She had run the whole way from the far end of the garden and was breathless. "Rosa and I have hunted everywhere and can't find her!"

"But that's rubbish! How could she possibly be gone? Rosa has been with the little ones the whole morning."

"Not all the morning." Jo was getting her breath back now. "She left them at half past ten to go and get their milk and biscuits. When she got to the kitchen, she found that Marie had scalded her hand rather badly, and stopped to tie it up for her. Then she had to pour out the milk, and she found that it was turning – the heat, you know. So she had to go to the cellar for more. She thinks she must have been gone at least twenty minutes, probably more. When she got back only Primula and the boys were there – Mamzelle had the rest in another part of the garden. She thought perhaps Sybil had begun to cry and Mamzelle had come to see what was wrong and taken her off. She gave Jackie and Bride and Primula their milk, and then went to see. Mamzelle said she'd seen nothing of the tinies since Frühstück. Then Primula and Bride began some rigmarole about 'Maria' coming and taking Sybil off. Rosa thought they meant Maria Marani – would you believe she could be so idiotic? – and that you'd sent her for Baby. She was just going to bring Jackie in when I landed, and we've been hunting like mad ever since. Oh, Madge! What does it mean? Maria Marani *hasn't* been here, has she?"

Madge Russell shook her head. "At this hour of the morning?" Then she broke off, for Rosa was coming up the path, carrying Jackie, and Primula Venables and Bride Bettany were trotting after her, tears pouring down their faces. Mamzelle, a pleasant Tyrolean of twenty-four or so, followed with the rest of the little flock. Rosa was crying, and Mamzelle looked very grave.

"Come and tell me what has happened," said Madge, controlling herself with an effort as she took Jackie from Rosa's arms. "Don't cry so, Rosa, Baby can't be far away."

Rosa choked down her sobs, and repeated her story, which was very much as Jo had retailed it. She had gone to bring the milk and biscuits, and coming back, had found Baby Sybil gone. When Jo came, she realized that there was something seriously wrong, and they had all hunted – to no avail. Nowhere could they find a cherubic baby girl with sapphire-blue eyes and coppery curls. The only clue they had was this tale of Bride's and Primula's about "Maria".

Madge guessed at once what had happened. Maria Balbini had come to the garden and carried off Baby

116

Sybil by way of avenging her own and her brother's fancied wrongs. She must be somewhere with the child. And Maria's mother was dying and asking for her own children, and they were not to be found!

For a moment, Madge Russell felt sick with horror. Then she woke up to the fact that Jo was shaking her gently and asking if Jem should be rung up.

"No," said Madge. "He couldn't come. Princess Balbini is dying, and I won't have him worried about this until it is absolutely necessary. But we must find those children. Be quiet, all of you, and let me think."

A hush fell, even the little ones being silent. Presently Madge looked up. "Rosa, take the children upstairs, and put them to bed. It is time they had their morning nap. Stay with them – don't leave them for a moment! Mamzelle, you go with her. Whatever happens, the children are not to be left. Do you understand?"

"Ja, Madame," sobbed Rosa.

Madge laid a slender hand on one of the heaving shoulders. "Don't cry, Rosa. It can do no good, and is only frightening the children. Do your duty by them, and pray that our Sybil may be safe."

Quieter at once, Rosa lifted Jackie who was drowsy and bore him off to the night nursery, followed by Mamzelle and the rest of the little band.

"What shall I do, Madge?" demanded Jo.

"Put a hat on, and then try the Maurach side. They *can't* have gone far. Sybil is a big, heavy child. If Maria tries to go far with her, she will soon find that she's undertaken more than she can manage."

"But there may be more than Maria in it," said Jo, voicing her fear. "There seem to be half a dozen of them, and they're in everything. They could take it in turns to

117

carry her. Sybil is accustomed to girls of that age, and would love to go with them."

"Not at this hour," said Sybil's mother, more experienced than Jo. "She's generally fast asleep by this time, and if they try to keep her awake, she'll roar and fight. And if you are right, Jo, and there are more in it than those twins, we ought to catch them soon. A crowd of children like that is noticeable. Ask everyone you meet. Call at the Gasthaus at Maurach and ask there."

"Right! What are you going to do?"

"See if they've tried to get up the mountain path anywhere. It's quite possible. But I feel sure they couldn't go far."

"What about the Seehof direction?"

"I've thought of that. They can't go any way but round by the path, so I'll ring up Herr Francke, and ask him to look out for them. Now go, Joey."

Jo paused only to bestow a rare kiss on her sister, and then grabbed her big, shady hat, and set off as hard as she could pelt down the road that leads by the eastern side of the mountain railway to the plain.

That was a dreadful morning. They hunted everywhere, but no sign of the missing children was to be found. No one had seen anything of them, though they learned that only the Balbini children and Mélanie Kerdec were missing. The others were all accounted for. Questioned, they all declared that, though they had known that Maria meant to kidnap the Russell baby, none of them knew where she intended taking her. Twice they were sent on false trails, only to find that the children described were farm children. Rosalie came in at thirteen o'clock, hot, tired, and dusty. She had hunted all round Seespitz, but had neither seen nor heard anything of them since ten o'clock that morning, when the twins had been seen playing by the lakeside. Madge, returned from a fruitless hunt up the mountainside, made her take some food and then go and lie down. Rosalie was not strong, and she looked worn out.

Jo returned an hour later, a sight to behold, since she had climbed in various directions, and fought her way through bushes in the vain hope that the children might be hiding behind them. Madge was at the telephone, answering a call from the sanatorium. As her sister entered she raised inquiring eyebrows, but Jo shook her head despairingly.

"Jo has just come in, Jem," said his wife. "She has no news."

She listened to the reply; answered, "Very well! Oh, Jem, I'm so *sorry*!" and then rang off.

"What does Jem want?" asked Jo, leaning against the doorpost, too listless to move.

"He rang up to ask if the children had been found." Madge slipped an arm round the girl. "Come, Joey – come to the salon and lie down. You can't do anything more at present."

Jo went with her sister. She sank down on the cane lounge, and sat there, playing idly with her hat. "What does Jem say, Madge?"

"The princess is sinking fast," said Madge gravely. "She is still conscious, and has asked for the children more than once. But that last rally was the final flicker. She is slipping away, and they can do nothing. Oh, those poor, silly children! What heartbreak they have stored up for themselves!"

Jo had been slumping. At these last words, she suddenly sat bolt upright. "Madge Russell! How can you?

119

Those little wretches have taken Sybil away, and goodness knows where they've got her! You are ill with worry about her, and then you call them 'poor'! For my part, I think they deserve everything that comes to them, and it's to be hoped their father gives them both a sound whipping. It's only what they deserve; and I wouldn't mind being the one to whip them, either!"

"Don't talk like that, Joey! When they think that their mother wanted them to say goodbye and they weren't there to give her her last wish, they're going to be hurt far more than by any whipping."

"It's their own fault," argued Jo, who was fractious with worry and fatigue.

"Yes," said Madge. "And that will make it worse."

"Oh, well, I always knew you were half an angel. I'm *not* – I'm human, and I haven't the least scrap of pity or sympathy for them!" snapped Jo. "I just hope they do suffer for this!"

"*Don't*, Joey!" Madge turned to the door. "Now slip off your shoes and put your feet up. I'm bringing you something to eat."

"Madge, I couldn't eat a thing! I'll rest, for I'm too dead to go on without. But *don't* bring me food! I shall be sick if you do!"

However, Madge refused to listen. She went away and returned with fruit salad and a glass of milk, and she insisted on Jo's finishing both. Then she darkened the room, and told the weary girl to sleep if she could.

"I'm going to ring up people round the lake. They *can't* have left it, or someone would have noticed them."

"No can't about it, apparently. They seem to have done it."

"There's only the Balbinis and little Mélanie Kerdec.

Those three aren't going far burdened with a big baby like Sybil. They are somewhere near the lake – probably quite near, if we could only get a clue."

Jo sat up. "Madge, you ought to tell Jem."

"Joey, I can't! He's with that poor woman, and he can't leave her."

"Why not? Jack Maynard is there, and so is Gottfried Mensch. If she is dying, I don't see what difference it makes whether he stays there or not."

But Madge had been a doctor's wife for four years, and she knew that as long as his patient had any need of him he would stay. So she refused to trouble him. Time enough when the Princess Balbini's sufferings were over.

So the afternoon passed, slowly and heavily. From the Briesau end came word that no one had heard anything of either the Balbini twins, Mélanie Kerdec, or Baby Sybil. Miss Annersley had sent out all mistresses who could be spared to hunt. Mamsell and Rosa left their charges in the hands of Mrs Russell and Rosalie Dene, and set off for Seehof. Joey, worn out, slept most of the time, greatly to her sister's relief. Jo had been a very delicate child, and even now could not stand much nervous strain. The Robin helped with the tinies, and kept them amused.

At sixteen o'clock, Jem rang up once more. Madge, who was never far from the telephone during those awful hours, answered it at once. She guessed his news.

"That you, Madge? Any news of those children?"

"None. How – how— "

"Gone," he said briefly. "She slipped away a quarter of an hour ago. Mercifully, she was unconscious for the last hour and a half. If those two turn up, keep them at St Scholastika's. They are too late to see their mother now; but their father will need them presently.

121

I'm coming down myself in half an hour, and if you've got them, I'll take them back with me – Madge! My darling, what's wrong?" For with the need to keep up before her husband ended, Madge Russell had sobbed uncontrollably.

"Oh, Jem!" Her voice shook. "Those children have taken Sybil, and we can't find them or her!"

"*What?*"

Madge repeated the statement. Then, in answer to his frenzied questions, she told him the story as briefly as possible. She was not always coherent, for reaction was coming now; but at length he had the full story, and then he issued his orders.

"You go and lie down till I come. I'll be with you as quickly as I can. Tell Jo to give you some wine and a decent meal – and *eat* it! Do you hear me? Jack can see to things here now. I'm coming at once, and I'll bring Rufus with me. Don't you worry, sweetheart! We'll have those little wretches before long! Do as I tell you!" And then he rang off. Jo, roused from her sleep by the voices – the doctor's last sentences were yelled – was just in time to see the receiver drop from her sister's nerveless hand, and spring forward to break her fall. The relief of knowing that her husband would be at hand to take the worst of the trouble on his broad shoulders had been too much for Madge, and even as he rang off, she fainted quietly away.

CHAPTER 11

Found!

How the doctor got down to the Tiernsee, neither he nor anyone else could tell after it was all over. He arrived, hot, dusty, and dishevelled, about half an hour after he had rung up. With him came Jo's great St Bernard, Rufus. By that time, Madge was in bed, having been put there by Joey and Rosa after she had recovered consciousness. She was as white as the pillows on which she lay, and the heavy shadows under her eyes told of her agony of mind; but she was quite calm when her husband bent over her.

"Not ill, dearest; only a headache. I'll be all right presently. You'll try to find the children at once, won't you? Never mind me; Jo can look after me."

"All right, sweetheart. I'll leave something for you to take, and Jo will give you it. Try not to worry. Those little demons can't have gone far with a kid of Sybil's weight – and temper! Luckily, it's warm enough, so she can't catch cold."

"Too warm!" said Madge's eyes as she thought of the tremendous heat which had poured down all day. That had been her great fear. If the children had been careless, her baby might suffer from sunstroke. But she said nothing to add to his anxiety.

Jen knew all about it, however, and called Jo out of the room for a moment. "Joey, I want you!" Then, as she shut the door behind her, and joined him at a window a little further along, he jerked out, "Had Baby anything on her head?"

"I couldn't tell you. Rosa would know," she replied.

Rosa was summoned, and informed them amid tears that Baby had been wearing a big print sunbonnet which had been securely tied on since she was in the habit of tearing off her headgear and throwing it down if it were loose.

"Thank God for that!" said Jem when he had dismissed Rosa again.

"You think—?" Jo could get no further for the lump in her throat.

"I don't think they would take it off," he said. "Now, Jo, I'll give you a sedative for Madge. See that she takes it, and then darken the room, and once she's asleep, leave her. She won't wake up for some hours. Then I'm going to the Seehaus for something belonging to those little demons, and we'll set Rufus to work."

Joey nodded. "It's a good idea. Shall I come for the sedative now?"

Struck by her tone, he swung her round to the light. "Let me look at you. H'm! You aren't in much better shape than Madge. Look here, Jo, I daren't put you to sleep, too. Someone must stay awake in case of need. Pull yourself together, Kiddy! I'm not afraid that Sybil will have to suffer more than inconvenience, I expect to find her dirty and hungry, and very cross; but nothing else. She's a sturdy youngster – hasn't ailed a bit all her days. The one thing I was afraid of was her head, but if her sunbonnet was tied on with one of Rosa's patent knots, they'd never have the patience to undo it; and I scarcely think they would dare to cut the strings. So that will be all right."

Jo smiled wanly. "I could believe anything of those imps. But surely, with Rufus, you'll get them soon. Oh, Jem!" She clung to him, sobbing noiselessly, and he held her fast for a moment. Then he put her from him. "No time for that now, Jo. Come for that draught, and when Madge is asleep, go and lie down yourself. Where's the rest of the nursery, by the way?"

"In the garden with Mamzelle and Rosalie," said Jo, struggling to recover herself. "You needn't worry about them, Jem."

"I know that. Now, come with me."

He led the way to his tiny dispensary, and mixed Jo a stiff dose of sal volatile before attending to the sedative for his wife. Then he sent the girl upstairs with it, sponged his hands and face, and, feeling fresher and fitter, called for Rufus, who was lying under the trees in the garden, and set off for the Seehaus, where he demanded Zia Emilia. She gave him a sock of Mario's and a little vest of Maria's, and would have detained him with questions about her brother, and her sister-in-law's death, but he put her off with a hasty, "Can't stop now! We must find those children at once. My wife is worrying herself into an illness over our little girl, and your brother will want his pair presently. Another time, if you please."

Then he was off, leaving her with half a dozen questions on her lips, and she retired to her own room to lament the wickedness of her niece and nephew, her sister-in-law's death, and her poor brother's sorrow.

Meanwhile, Dr Jem had shown the articles to Rufus, and bidden him track their owners. The big dog promptly began to nose the ground, and after some difficulty, got on to the scent, and set off at a pace which made the doctor trot to keep up with him. To St Scholastika's he

125

went, where he turned sharply to the left, and passing down the back of the place, reached a thin part in the hedge through which he tried to push.

Guessing that this was where Maria had broken in, the doctor tugged him off, and led him a little further along, where the great dog once more picked up the scent, and was off again, down the valley towards Maurach. Dr Jem, towed along at the other end of his chain, had hard work to keep up with the long, swinging paddy-pad – paddy-pad which was Rufus' steady pace.

At the place where the footpath up the Sonnalpe begins, there came a hail, and looking up the doctor saw one of his colleagues scrambling down towards him.

"Gottfried!" he exclaimed. "What in the world—!"

"Joey rang me up," gasped Gottfried Mensch, mopping his brow. "She asked me to come and help you if I could. I told Gisela, and came at once. Jack is in charge, and Gray has just come up. We have got that poor fellow to take some food and then lie down for a rest; but the one thing he wants is his children. We have said nothing about Sybil, of course. He thinks the children are having a picnic, and Jack will see that he hears nothing else at present. Has Rufus got the scent?"

"Yes; at least, it looks like it. Thanks for coming, Gottfried. It may be just as well if there is more than one of us. I wouldn't trust that precious pair as far as I could throw them! And Sybil will have to be carried, of course."

The tall, fair young doctor, younger by a good eight years than his chief, nodded. "So I thought. If you were carrying Sybil, it would be a job to control the Balbini imps."

"But where on earth have they gone?" exclaimed the

126

elder man. "I should never have believed that two children could have come so far carrying a heavy child like Sybil!"

"There were three of them, though," said Gottfried. "Jo said that the Kerdec child was with them."

"So she was. But Mélanie Kerdec would prove a very broken reed to lean on, I imagine."

"Still, she could help with the carrying," his colleague reminded him. "Ah! Rufus has stopped and is circling. The scent breaks here."

Break it did. They took Rufus some yards further in all directions, but he was unable to pick it up again. Dr Russell looked serious. What could have happened to the children?

Gottfried Mensch, fresher, and not quite so anxious, guessed at once what had happened. "Someone with a car or donkey has come along and they have begged a lift," he said.

"Good Heavens! Then they may be anywhere!" exploded the doctor.

Gottfried nodded. "You'd better try the Polizei, Jem."

"It begins to look as if I must." The doctor frowned, while Rufus nosed his hand gently.

"What about going to the Maurach Gasthaus and telephoning from there?" suggested Gottfried.

"Yes; that would be best," replied Jem. "But I'm thankful to remember, Gottfried, that I've given my wife a sleeping draught, and she is not likely to wake up for five or six hours. By that time we ought to have some news of them. I only wish I had the little fiends here! I could wring their young necks for this!"

Gottfried said nothing, and the two men with the great dog went on to Maurach, where they tried to enter

127

the Gasthaus, only to be warned off by a policeman who suddenly appeared.

"Nein, mein Herrn! Nobody may enter here."

"Why not?" demanded Gottfried Mensch.

The man was only too eager to tell them. "One of the servants is ill with smallpox," he informed them. "She came up from Innsbruck only two days ago. She has been sick and poorly, and this morning the rash appeared. Frau Erzing sent to the Sonnalpe for a doctor, who has just gone a short while ago, and he pronounced it smallpox, and said that none were to enter, and none to leave."

"Gray," murmured Jem Russell in an undertone. "I remember, he was sent for about noon. Look here, Gottfried, you'd better get back for his report. Jack will be on duty at the sanatorium."

"And the children?"

"I'll see to the children. You get off."

Gottfried nodded. "Ring for me if I am wanted. Good luck, Jem!" And he turned and went back up the mountainside.

Dr Russell turned once more to the man to ask if he had seen anything of the children. And here, at last, he got news. Yes; the children had been seen. There were three dark little ones, and a baby who yelled, and would not be comforted. They had been seen one – two hours ago.

Hope leapt up in Jem's heart. "Where were they?"

"They were coming down the road, mein Herr. They were trying to carry the baby, but she fought with them, and cried loudly – *very* loudly," he added, reflectively.

Worried as he was, Jem grinned. He had had some experience of his daughter's yells when she was in a regular paddy. "Where did they go?" he asked.

"A lady and gentleman in a big red car stopped and spoke to them, and took them in, and whirled away. They were English, for on the car I saw the letters GB."

"Did you notice the number?"

"Ja, mein Herr. It was LCJ 1076. It was a very large car."

British; and obviously moneyed people. They would see that the older children were not English, and Sybil would most certainly prove herself of another nationality, since she spoke English with an odd word or two of German. What could these children be doing together like this? Surely they would smell a rat! Then it occurred to Jem to wonder why Jo had heard nothing of all this. But, as later transpired, it had happened after she had been at Maurach; and as for the smallpox, she had gone to the nearer Gasthaus, and had heard of the case, but the anxiety over Sybil completely drove it out of her mind. But here, at last, was news. Where the children could have been during the morning was a mystery at present. But now there seemed every chance of catching up with them. Jem looked round, and considered.

Across the stillness of the hot afternoon came the delirious whistling of the tiny mountain train which linked up the lakeside with the world on the plain below. He made up his mind, and bidding adieu to the guard, and followed by Rufus, raced across the track to the station, determined to catch the train back to the Tiernsee, and get to the nearest telephone, whence he could notify the police at Spärtz. He was just in time to reach the station when, with a wild screech, the engine came round the bend and drew up. The little open carriages were very full. A few people descended, evidently bound for one or other of the Gasthäuser. Jem's duty was to warn them away from the infected one; but he paid no heed to his duty. His eyes were glued to a compartment in which sat a big, bearded man, a small, sunbonneted creature in his arms; on the seat in front of him sat two little girls and a boy.

Jem made a wild leap, and crowded into the compartment, heedless of cries that they were full up, and there was no room. Rufus hurled himself after him, and the noise was tremendous. But the doctor took no notice. Bending over the burly man, he snatched the baby from him.

She turned a dirty, tear-stained little face to him. Then she uttered a rapturous cry of: "Dad-dad!" and flung her arms round him. The children in front turned horror-stricken faces to them, and the smaller of the girls burst into tears. The big man crushed himself against the side of the compartment, and indicated the three inches or so of seat thus left vacant.

"Sit down, my dear fellow," he said in German. "You will see I have brought back the truants. I met them in Spärtz and recognized my goddaughter. As I knew such young Taugenichtsen had no right to be there with her, I arrested the lot, and soon got some sort of story from them. I would have rung you up, but my telephone is out of order, and I thought the quickest way would be to bring them all back by the next train. They were not sorry, I fancy," he added with a twinkle. "My goddaughter has not behaved as a little lady should, I fear."

Hugging his precious small daughter, Jem answered, "Thanks, Anserl, more than I can say. My wife has suffered agonies on Sybil's behalf. She knew I was needed at the sanatorium – a patient dying – so would not send for me until all was over. Then she broke down completely, so I gave her a sedative, and she will be sleeping now."

Herr Anserl nodded. "And these?" he asked, indicating the children in front with a nod.

"They have brought about their own punishment," said Jem gravely, as he tried to restrain Sybil from strangling him by tugging at his collar. "Don't, Baby! Lie still, my pet! Mélanie comes out of it – unless her people punish her for running away like this," he added, with a glance at the weeping Mélanie. "But the other two – look here, Anserl; when we stop, grab them. I can't have them going off now. They must come along to St Scholastika's with us. Ah, here we are!" as the engine once more made violent efforts to burst itself while it swept across the little plain, and clanked to a stop before the Seespitz hut. "Keep hold of the Balbini children."

Herr Anserl placed a heavy hand on a shoulder of either twin, just as they were meditating an escape by climbing over the open side of the compartment. The passengers gradually left, casting curious glances at the little group which remained sitting. Then Jem got out, holding Sybil closely, to find Miss Annersley and all the prefects awaiting him. They surrounded him and his daughter, so he handed the young lady over to her future Headmistress, and turned to see about the other children, while the girls crowded round with exclamations of joy. Sybil resented it all. She was hot, tired, and hungry, and in what her aunt would have called "a thoroughgoing red-haired temper". So she struck out at them all, and yelled lustily, till Miss Annersley, with Louise at the wheel, got into the school car with her, and drove off to St Scholastika's, where the prodigal was received with a rapturous welcome which made her

131

crosser than ever, until Rosa bore her off to bed, bath, and supper.

Meanwhile, Herr Anserl had ordered the sobbing Mélanie out of the compartment, followed her, holding Maria's arm, and, when the doctor had taken charge of the latter young lady, lifted Mario down, and kept hold of him.

"What now?" demanded the old music master.

Jem looked round. Then he gave a shout. "There's Gottfried with the runabout. Come on! We'll get them to St Scholastika's! You girls," he turned to the laughing girls who were surrounding them, "get back to school out of this heat, and try to keep quiet. Now then, Anserl, can you get in at the back with Mélanie and Maria? I'll keep this young man." And he gave the unwilling Mario a little pull in the direction of the car.

The Chaletians dispersed with joyous goodbyes. Gottfried held Maria until Herr Anserl had hoisted himself up into the dickey with Mélanie beside him. Then Maria was handed up, and sat on the big Tyrolean's knee, while Jem and Mario squeezed into the seat beside the driver.

It was a good thing that Gottfried was an excellent driver. He got his crowded car safely to St Scholastika's, where Jo was at the door to welcome them, and the three truants were taken out and marched to the salon, Herr Anserl retaining his grip on the twins.

"You may go back to the hotel, Mélanie," said Dr Russell after he had heard that Sybil was safely in the nursery with Rosa. "I expect you will. be punished for running off like this – I know you had very little to do with kidnapping Sybil, so we'll say nothing more about it. But I'm afraid your mother is exceedingly angry with you."

132

Mélanie was weeping like a waterspout already; but at this, she uttered a howl which outdid Sybil's best efforts in the line. Miss Annersley, who had waited in case they needed help with the twins, was sorry for her, and looked a question at the doctor. He nodded.

"Yes; take her back, and see if you can gain a slight remission of her punishment. I don't blame her half so much as the other two. She's clay in their hands, I fancy. You might tell Madame Kerdec as much."

The Head took the hot, sticky paw, and drew Mélanie out to the school car. Then the doctor sat down, and Herr Anserl, still holding the twins in a firm grasp, brought them before him.

"Where have you been all day?" he asked abruptly.

"That is our business," said Maria curtly.

"Did you know that the whole valley has been looking for you ever since noon?"

No answer; but a little grin edged Mario's lips at this information. It vanished the next instant, however, as the doctor added gravely, "Your mother wanted you both. I rang up at noon for you, but you were not to be found."

"But we must go!" cried Maria, struggling like a wild thing in Herr Anserl's grasp. "If Mamma wants us – "

"You are too late now, Maria," said Jem Russell very gently. "She does not want you now."

Something in his voice struck the child. She stood still, terror slowly filling her proud little face. "What do you mean?"

"You are too late, my child. She does not want you – she will never again on this earth ask for you."

The children looked at him wildly. They were beginning to understand, but they fought against the knowledge.

133

"Listen," he said, a stern kindness in his tones. "When your mother asked for you, it was to say goodbye to you, for she was dying. You were not to be found, though many people have been looking for you all these hours. We have got you at last – but too late. Your mother died at half past fifteen."

"It's a lie!" Maria was nearly beside herself. "You are trying to punish us by frightening us! Oh, I know we stole your baby – we meant to hurt your horrid wife, and I hope we did! I heard you say she was ill, and I'm glad! But it's cruel to say such things to us to punish us!"

"It would be very cruel if I did such a thing," agreed the doctor. "Unfortunately, Maria, your foolish behaviour has brought its own punishment. Your mother asked for you repeatedly before she died, and she had to go with her last wish for you ungratified. You will always remember that. And the pity of it is that it need never have been."

There was silence. Mario seemed stunned by the awful news, and his twin was still fighting desperately against belief in it. It *couldn't* be that they were to be punished like that! God couldn't be so cruel! Maria rarely spoke of her mother, but she had a passionate love for her all the same. Oh, God *couldn't* have done that to them, even though they had been so very wicked! Then something in the deep pity, almost tenderness she saw in the grave blue eyes of the doctor told her that it *was* true. With a scream which those who heard it remembered for months, the child flung up her arms, and, but for Herr Anserl's hold on her, would have dropped to the floor. Jo, nearest of all, caught her from the music master, and lowered her gently. Then, as Jem dropped on his knees beside the unconscious child, she caught sight of Mario's face, and flung her arms round him.

"Oh, you poor little man!" she cried. "Don't look like that! Maria isn't dead – only fainted. She'll be all right in a minute."

The boy felt the comfort of her arms, and flung his own round her. Clinging to her, he burst into long, shuddering sobs, and Jo had her hands full with him for the next few minutes.

By the time they had brought Maria round, and forced some milk into her, it was twenty o'clock, and Jem decided against taking the children to the Sonnalpe that night. Both were worn out; Maria, indeed, seemed on the verge of an illness, and bed was the best thing for them. Mario, who had sobbed out his first grief in Jo's kind arms, was drowsy, and the doctor almost undressed him before he laid him in the little camp bed set up in his own dressing room. Jo and Rosalie attended to Maria, who was put into the room opening from Jo's, the Robin being banished to the night nursery for once.

Jem came along after seeing Mario safely into bed, and nodded to Jo to leave him with the little girl; so she slipped along to the night nursery to bend over Sybil, who lay spreadeagled across her cot in her usual fashion, long black lashes sweeping rosy cheeks, cherubic expression in full force. She seemed to have taken no harm from her adventure, and was sleeping as peacefully as usual.

Jo left the crib, and went to kiss the Robin good night at the other side of the big room. It was well past the small girl's bedtime, so neither spoke. Besides, the other babies might have been roused. Then the girl left the room, with a subdued Rosa sitting in one corner beside a shaded lamp, knitting as if her life depended on it, and slipped into the big, airy room where she found her sister waking up. She was still heavy with the drug

135

Jem had given her, but at sight of Joey, remembrance came back.

"Joey! My baby!" she cried.

"Fast asleep, all over her cot as usual," said Jo cheerfully. "Those young imps had got her to Maurach, where they begged a lift from someone, and so reached Spärtz. Luckily, good old Vater Bär met them, and he captured them, and was bringing all back when Jem boarded the train at Maurach – *plus* Rufus, who seems to have created a small sensation. Baby was brought safely home, bathed, fed, and is now fast asleep, and looking as well as ever she did. Miss Annersley, meantime, marched Mélanie off to the Seehaus, where, so I gather, an irate mamma caned her soundly for going off like that, and put her to bed on bread and milk. However, the Abbess has pleaded for her forgiveness, so they're going to say no more."

"And the Balbini twins?" asked Madge.

"Here," said Jo gravely. "Jem has broken the news to them, and the shock has been rather too much for them – Where are you going?" For Madge had flung back the sheets, and was getting out of bed.

"To see Baby first, and then do what I can for those poor children."

"Indeed you aren't!" A masculine voice spoke emphatically from the doorway. "You're going to stay where you are, my dear. Jo can bring Baby to you if you want her. But you don't leave this room till noon tomorrow. Remember that! Jo, you run and bring Baby here."

Jo went, and returned, carrying a still sleeping Sybil. She put the red-curled creature into her mother's arms, and left them together with the remark, "Don't worry about the Balbini twins. I'll see to them."

"Jo is worth her weight in gold," remarked the doctor

136

as he settled his wife comfortably. "You stay where you are, sweetheart, and cuddle Baby. Marie will bring you something to eat later, and then try to go to sleep again. I'll be up later on. I'll stay down tonight as it's so late."

He went off to seek his wife's supper, and Madge, still drowsy, cuddled down, and was soon asleep again.

Meanwhile, Jo, passing along the corridor and thinking longingly of bed, heard low moans proceeding from Maria's room. She pushed open the door and entered quietly. It was full moon, so there was no need for other light. Jo bent over the little bed, and drew back the clothes. Maria Balbini, with wild eyes in a white face, looked up at her.

"Why have you come?" she gasped.

"To see you," said Jo, sitting down on the side of the bed, and taking the child in her arms.

"Say it isn't true!" gasped Maria, clinging to her convulsively. "Say it isn't true!"

"I can't do that, Maria. God has called your mother, and she has gone. She'll never have any more pain or weakness or sorrow. She will always be well now. It's very dreadful for you, but won't you try to remember what a wonderful thing it is for her?"

"She *can't* be dead – she *can't* be!"

Jo said nothing, but held the child closely while she shook with a paroxysm of sobbing. Presently she grew calmer. "If only I could tell her how sorry I am!" she gasped.

"She knows, and forgives you," said Jo simply.

"Are you sure? Oh, are you *sure*?"

"I'm certain!" And such was the confidence in Jo's voice that the overwrought child reacted to it at once. She lay against the older girl's shoulder, almost calm.

Presently she looked up. "Will – will God forgive us?"

"Yes; if you're truly sorry, and try to make amends for what you've done."

"How can we? We can't make Signora Russell well again."

"No; though she's much better now she knows that Sybil is safe. But you can do it in other ways. Your father will need you. You will have to try to comfort him for his terrible loss. No one can do it better than you two, for you are his children. Maria, you must be well and strong tomorrow, so that you can go up to the Sonnalpe to him. You can only do that if you sleep. Close your eyes, now, and I'll sing you to sleep as I've sung Robin many a time."

Influenced by something she could not understand, Maria obediently shut her eyes, and lay in Jo's arms, quite still, while Jo, sitting there in the moonlight, the little black head with its wild scatter of long curls against her shoulder, opened her mouth and sang, with a voice as sweet and fresh as a young-eyed seraph's, "The Shepherd's Cradle-Song".

She felt the weary little figure in her arms relax as she sang the third verse, and when she ended her song, she knew that Maria was asleep. Rising carefully, she laid the child down and covered her up. Then she turned to see her brother-in-law at the door.

"Thanks, Joey. That's probably saved her a bad illness," he murmured as he came to bend over Maria. "She'll be all right, now she's got to sleep." He rose, and drew the girl out of the room with him. "And now, Joey, proud as I am of you for the way you've behaved today, I think I've seen enough of you for once. Off to bed with you, and let me hear nothing more of you till morning!" But his kiss was very tender as he held her for a moment before pushing her into her own room.

"You're none too beautiful yourself!" retorted Jo from the doorway. "I'd advise you to take a dekko at yourself in the nearest mirror. And ask Marie to send me some milk and bread and butter up, will you? I've just discovered I'm hungry. Tell her not to stint."

The doctor went off laughing to give the order. But he carefully refrained from examining his appearance in the mirror until he had had a meal and a bath before turning in. Then he grinned at himself in his shaving glass, murmuring, "Jo is a cheeky youngster. But she's turned up trumps today, if ever a girl did!"

The Chalet School
Series
ELINOR M. BRENT-DYER

Elinor M. Brent-Dyer has written many books about life at the famous alpine school. Follow the thrilling adventures of Joey, Mary-Lou and all the other well-loved characters in these delightful stories, available only in Armada.

ARMADA

Other titles by
Enid Blyton
in Armada

ARMADA

Nancy Drew
Mystery Stories

Nancy Drew is the best-known and most-loved girl detective ever. Join her and her best friends, George Fayne and Bess Marvin, in her many thrilling adventures available in Armada.

ARMADA

Other titles by
Enid Blyton
in Armada

ARMADA

All these books are available at your local bookshop or newsagent, or can be ordered from the publisher. To order direct from the publishers just tick the title you want and fill in the form below:

Name _____

Address _____

_____

Send to: Collins Childrens Cash Sales
PO Box 11
Falmouth
Cornwall
TR10 9EN

Please enclose a cheque or postal order or debit my Visa/Access –

Credit card no:

Expiry date:

Signature:

– to the value of the cover price plus:

UK: 60p for the first book, 25p for the second book, plus 15p per copy for each additional book ordered to a maximum charge of £1.90.

BFPO: 60p for the first book, 25p for the second book plus 15p per copy for the next 7 books, thereafter 9p per book.

Overseas and Eire: £1.25 for the first book, 75p for the second book. Thereafter 28p per book.

ARMADA